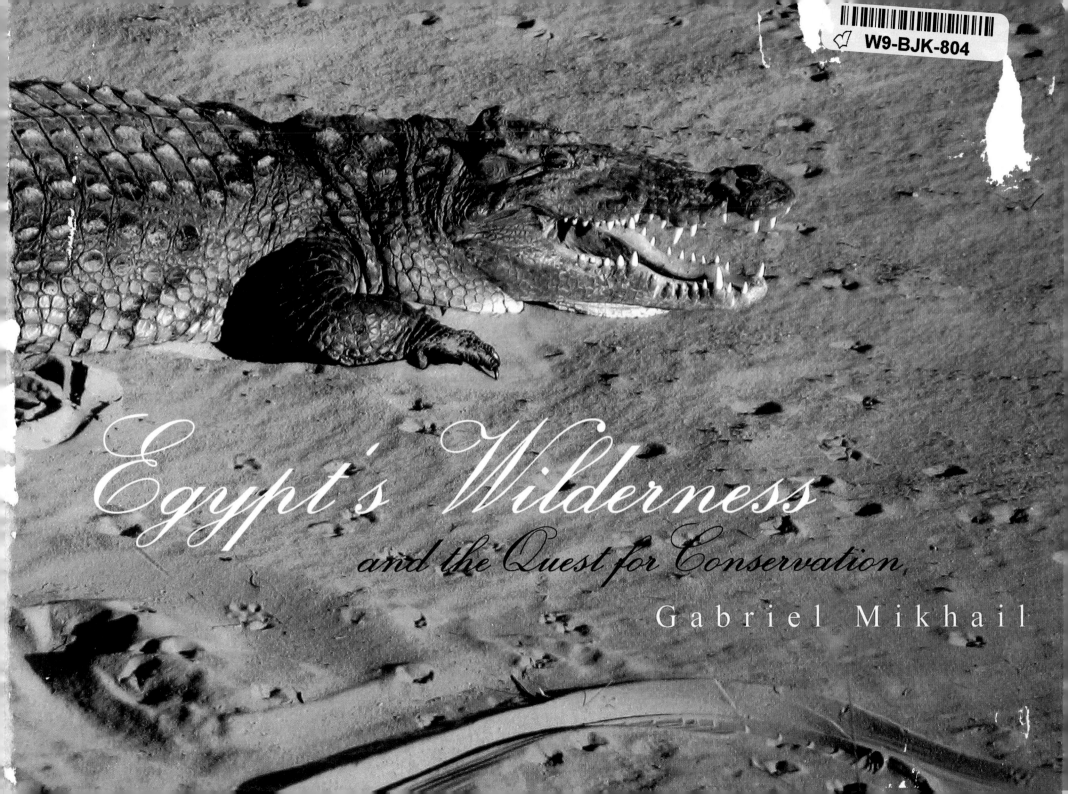

Egypt's Wilderness

and the Quest for Conservation

Gabriel Mikhail

Preface

Egypt is blessed with a wide variety of species and ecosystems that contribute to the health, well being and prosperity of its people. In order to preserve these precious and invaluable treasures that it possesses, Egypt has adopted policies, plans and programs to protect its unique natural heritage and accomplish its commitments towards the international agreements to which it is signatory.

Protected areas are Egypt's indispensable tools for the conservation of nature. The sound and effective management of these areas has been one of the major concerns of the Ministry of State for Environmental Affairs / Egyptian Environmental Affairs Agency over the past ten years. Economic viability of nature conservation efforts is also important if they are to remain sustainable on the long run. Several national initiatives are undertaken for the valuation of protected areas and their potential contribution to the economic growth of the country, especially in relation to ecotourism; inclusion of protected areas in the National Investment and Land Use Map of Egypt; and the implementation of proper and adequate management plans in all protected areas.

Finally, I would like to express my appreciation to the Ministry of Environment and to the Egyptian Environmental Affairs Agency for their diligent efforts and apparent achievements in the field of nature conservation and sustainability of natural resources; including, inter-alia, the support of valuable documentations as portrayed in this publication.

Dr. Atef Ebeid
Prime Minister, EGYPT

Introduction

Egypt's natural heritage is rich with a wide diversity of ecosystems, rendering it unique worldwide. In this respect, and in accordance to Law 102 of 1983 for the preservation of natural resources and protectorates, the Ministry of State for Environmental Affairs has declared 24 protected areas covering some 91,000 km² and representing about 9% of the total nation's territory. It is planned to further expand this network to become comprehensively representative of all of Egypt's natural habitats and ecosystems, and to include a total of 40 protected areas, covering 15-17 % of the nation's area by the year 2017.

The effective management of these areas is the primary objective and focus of the Egyptian Environmental Affairs Agency. Correspondingly, initiatives were designed and implemented to ensure the sustainable utilization of these sites and their resources through a variety of means such as the promotion of eco-tourism, partnerships with local communities and raising public awareness.

I would like to express our appreciation to the European Commission for its support and cooperation in protecting our natural resources and biodiversity. Special tribute is due to Professor Mohamed A. Kassas and Dr. Loutfy Boulos for their indispensable guidance and counsel. We also thank Dr. Mostafa Fouda for his initiative in the creation of this booklet. Dr. Sherif Baha El-Din, Dr. Lynn Mortensen and Dr. John Grainger have all made very positive contributions. Thanks to Ms Patsy Gasperetti for the compilation and editing of this document. Last but not least, special thanks to Gabriel Mikhail, the author and publisher of this book, for his remarkably talented work.

Dr. Mamdouh Riad
Minister of State for Environmental Affairs

Contents

Significance of Egypt's cultural and natural diversity 04

Diversity of species 05

Eco-zones of Egypt (facing page).............................. 06

A few of the endangered species in Egypt 34

Indigenous people 36

Medicinal plants 37

Local cultures in Egypt's diverse landscape 38

The Nature Conservation Sector (NCS)........................ 46

Protected areas.. 47

Conservation programs 52

Other NCS activities 54

Egypt's future conservation agenda 55

References 56

Artwork, paintings and photography by Gabriel Mikhail: 296 pictures
Contributions by other photographers:
Dr. Sherif Baha El-Din: 6 pictures, Dr. Omar Attum: 6 pictures,
Dina & Rafik Khalil: 4 pictures, Waheed Salama 1 picture.
Ras Mohamed National Park Archives: 4 pictures.
Saint Katherine Protectorate Archives: 6 pictures.

Marine photography by:
RAC/SPA's' publication: 10 pictures
Hagen Schmid & associates: 9 pictures.
Uwa & Nikola Jonitz: 2 pictures.

Gebel Elba 06

Mediterranean Wetlands 20

Mountains and Wadis of the Eastern Desert 08

The Nile Valley and Delta 22

Red Sea Littoral Habitats 10

Gabal Uweinat and Gilf Kebir 24

Red Sea Islands 12

Sand and Dunes of the Western Desert 26

Red Sea Marine Habitats 14

Western Desert Depressions and Oases 28

Mountains and Wadis of South Sinai 16

The W. Desert Mediterranean Coastal Zone 30

Central and North Sinai 18

Mediterranean Marine Habitats 32

Egypt, lies at the northeast corner of Africa at the junction of four biogeographical regions, Irano-Turanian, Mediterranean, Saharo-Sindian and Afrotropical. At the same time it is at the center of the great Saharo-Sindian desert belt that runs from Morocco on the northwest corner of Africa to the high, cold deserts of central Asia. Egypt is bounded on the north and east by two largely enclosed seas, the Mediterranean Sea and the Red Sea. This unique position is enhanced by the circumstance that it is divided by the Nile, the longest river in the world. Most of Egypt is either arid or hyper arid, however, due to its very varied eco-zones, the country is home to a wide diversity of terrestrial habitats and a fauna and flora, which although relatively low in species numbers and with few endemics, is extremely varied in composition.

Egypt was traversed by migratory peoples since time immemorial; some of them have settled in this ancient land and each group has influenced the landscape in its own way. Their indigenous knowledge and traditions constitute an important portion of Egypt's cultural heritage, which is largely eclipsed by the wonders of Ancient Egypt and its grand tombs, pyramids and temples. These cultures are also threatened by the intrusion of modern civilization. Promoting the welfare of these people not only conserves their unique knowledge and culture but also leads to the conservation of nature.

Similarly, ecosystems and habitats must be maintained to safeguard species. Species must be protected in order to conserve ecosystems and habitats. In Egypt, the fairly low number of species and the relatively large number of eco-zones and habitats makes the preservation of both especially important.

What biodiversity is about

Biodiversity is the numbers and diversity of plant and animal life together with genetic diversity and assemblages of organisms. However, biodiversity is much more than numbers of plants and animals, it is what underpins human life and well-being.

The concept of biodiversity is so broad that it reflects the linkages between genes, species and ecosystems. Therefore, whether wildlife products or services from ecosystems are required or whether the aim is merely to protect ecosystems for posterity, these linkages must be reflected in the way humans manage the world.

The significance of biodiversity is seen particularly well at species level. Species provide the food we eat, the plants from which much of the world's medicine comes, the clothes we wear, the trees that re-oxygenate the air we breath and many more benefits.

Genes provide the variations that make the system strong. For thousands of years man has recognized the importance of genetics in adapting plants to grow in such a way as to increase their yield and of breeding domestic animals to encourage the development of healthy animals with the most desirable characteristics for their purpose. Sound breeding policies increase the value of production significantly.

Ecosystems provide the habitats in which species can thrive. Coastal wetlands and the plants that live there, form spawning grounds for fish and crustaceans. Forest ecosystems help to regulate water runoff into rivers and to prevent flooding. The Amazon rainforest influences global climate while the presence or absence of vegetation can influence climate locally. The list is almost endless.

**Egypt lies at the junction of four bio-geographical regions.
At the same time it is at the center of the great Saharo-Sindian desert.**

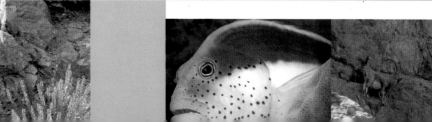

Diversity of species

The numbers in the table below include only those species that have been documented.

Taxa		No. of species	Notes
FLORA			
Bryophyta		337	Liverworts and mosses
Pteridophyta		16	Non-flowering vascular plants
Spermatophyta: Gymnospermae		6	Plants with no protective casing on the seeds
Angiospermae		2072	Flowering plants; 62 endemic species.
TERRESTRIAL FAUNA			
Invertebrata:	Insecta	10000	New study estimates ± 15000 species.
	Arachnida	1517	Mostly spiders, mites and ticks including 24 scorpion species
Vertebrata:	Amphibia	9	Including 1 endemic species
	Reptilia	97	Including 6 endemic and 1 endangered species
	Aves	470	Resident breeders 150; Migratory and wintering 320
	Mammalia	95	Including 6 endemic and 20 endangered species
MARINE FAUNA			
Invertebrata		1740	This is an extremely low estimate
Vertebrata:	Fish(Chondrichthyes & Osteichthyes)	669	This is an extremely low estimate
	Reptilia (turtles)	5	All five species of turtles are endangered
	Mammalia	14	Additionally, the Monk Seal and the Killer Whale may be found
FRESHWATER FAUNA			
Invertebrata		124	A low estimate
Vertebrata:	Fish (Osteichthyes)	70	Fifteen species have become extinct in the last century
	Reptilia	2	The Nile Crocodile and the Nile Soft-shelled Turtle

Gebel Elba

Gebel Elba at 1437m is far from being the highest of the group of mountains that overlooks the Red Sea but because of its unique attributes it is the most important area for flora and fauna in Egypt and is the centerpiece of the Elba Protected Area, which covers an area of approximately 35,600km² in the most southeasterly corner of Egypt.

Although rainfall on Gebel Elba averages only 50mm, its location facing the sea and its elevation increases annual precipitation to as much as 400mm on its upper reaches. Moist air from the Red Sea condenses on the peak of the mountain creating a mist oasis in which much of the moisture is dew and mist. The coast curves slightly to the east at this point, thus Gebel Elba presents an unusually broad front to the sea across a 20 – 25km strip of relatively flat land. The whole of the mountain is dissected by small wadis; these drain into larger wadis that eventually debouch into the plains below. Wadi Yahameib and Wadi Aidieb drain the north and northeast flanks of Gebel Elba and several species of *Acacia* form dense woods in their lower reaches, supported by the moisture from above. On its southern side the principal drainage is into Wadi Serimtai, which is characterized by open *Acacia* scrub.

The amount of available moisture is reflected in the flora and fauna on this mountain, which has the richest biodiversity of any area of comparable size in Egypt. A surprising number of the species found on Gebel Elba are not found anywhere else in Egypt and are mostly formed of Afrotropical elements for which this mountain is the northernmost limit. The flora consists of nearly 500 species, of which cryptogams (ferns and mosses) are fairly common at higher elevations. Among these are the delicate *Anogramma leptophylla*, which can be found in shady rock fissures and the well-known Maidenhair fern, *Adiantum capillus-veneris*, distinguished by its polished black stipes (stems) and delicate fronds. This little fern grows near water in warm temperate and sub-tropical areas of the world and was used by the Ancient Greeks to treat coughs. At least one species of plant (*Biscutella elbensis*) is endemic. The Ombet tree, *Dracaena ombet*, is found in Egypt, only on the higher slopes of Gebel Elba. The Ombet is a rather small tree related to the famous Dragon Tree of the Far East and when its rosettes of sword-like leaves are crowned with 30cm-long clusters of pink flowers it presents a truly dramatic appearance.

The Gebel Elba Snake-eyed Lizard, *Ophisops elbaensis*, is a strikingly colored lizard that was originally thought to be endemic to Gebel Elba but has since been found in the Arabian Peninsula. In Egypt it is restricted to this area as is Dodson's Toad, *Bufo dodsoni*. The deadly Saw-scaled Viper, *Echis pyramidum*, is also found in the area.

Two of the mammals found in the area, the Zoril, *Ictonyx striatus*, and the Aardwolf, *Proteles cristatus*, are sub-Saharan species. The Barbary Sheep, *Ammotragus lervia*, which was thought to be extinct in the Eastern Desert has recently been found to be extant in the area and in recent years fresh pugmarks of the Leopard, *Panthera pardus pardus*, have been seen. The mountain has been identified by BirdLife International as one of the Important Bird Areas (IBAs) of Egypt due to the high proportion of breeding birds found there. Many of these birds are either Afrotropical species or have disappeared from their former range in North Africa and the Middle East. Among them is the attractive red-breasted Rosy-patched Shrike, *Rhodophoneus cruentus*, which is found nowhere else in Egypt.

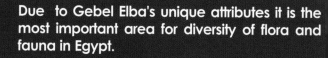

Due to Gebel Elba's unique attributes it is the most important area for diversity of flora and fauna in Egypt.

Lappet-faced Vulture, *Torgos tracheliotus*: Juvenile in nest. The adult of this bird of prey has a wingspan of up to three meters. A species associated with the Upper Egyptian goddess, *Nekhbet*, protector of the king. This species has declined over the centuries and has disappeared from many parts of the country.

Sand Partridge, *Ammoperdix heyi*: A denizen of rocky slopes and hills that has its global distribution mainly round the Red Sea. The mother and chicks can seem to disappear when they are in the safety of their rocky habitat where the nest is on the ground under an overhanging rock or bush. Sexes differ in coloration as the male is more brightly colored.

Nubian Nightjar, *Caprimulgus nubicus*: In Egypt, this nocturnal, insectivorous bird is found only in the Gebel Elba area. At night it may be seen gliding and wheeling after flying insects. By day it roosts on the ground near low vegetation and flies only if disturbed. Its rather dull coloration acts as an excellent camouflage and while it remains unmoving it is virtually invisible.

Wild Ass, *Equus asinus*: A slenderly built animal with large ears, a short upright mane and a long tufted tail. Sometimes with stripes on the legs. The status of these animals is uncertain owing to hybridization, however, their extreme agility and their speed on rough terrain has little to do with domestic donkeys. The pharaoh, *Ramesses III*, is said to have hunted them.

Gray's Agama, *Agama spinosa*: A typical lizard of the rocky lower slopes of wadis that is found throughout the Eastern Desert and changes color according to the temperature and its degree of activity. When cold it is rather dull in color, becoming more colorful when warm and active. Breeding males are more brightly colored than females, which have bluish heads and red bodies.

Ombet Tree, *Dracaena ombet*: This small but dramatic tree is found, in Egypt, only on the higher reaches of Gebel Elba. It grows up to five meters and its many forked branches are crowned with sword-shaped leaves that form dense rosettes. Its pink flowers grow in long erect clusters. It has been listed by the World Conservation Union (IUCN) as an endangered species.

The **Eastern Desert** that lies between the Nile Valley and the Red Sea is so different from the Western Desert that it seems odd to use the same word for both. This desert, although it has its share of sand, is dominated by its spine of rugged mountains seamed with wadis that support one of the richest assemblages of flora and fauna on mainland Egypt. Gebel Shayib El Banat (2187m) is the highest of a number of high mountain peaks some of which enjoy a degree of orographic precipitation, which creates mist oases. In addition to this, there is rainfall of less than 50mm annually. Run-off from the precipitation benefits the wadis and although there are no permanent watercourses, some water is retained and appears as springs; after a rare spell of rain pools form in rock basins.

On the eastern side of the mountains the many wadis are relatively short and steep, while on the west they are longer and less steep. Owing to the overall extreme aridity of the Eastern Desert, plant and animal life is generally restricted to the wadis and more specifically to the wadi sides. Because rain on the mountains drains into the wadi systems it tends to do so in the form of torrential floods. These floods not only carry with them rocks, sometimes very large ones, but anything growing that happens to be in their way. Because of this the main wadi channels are usually devoid of plant life and vegetation becomes established on the wadi banks above flood level. The exception is that in the lower reaches of wadis where they spread out and are less steep, any flood that has occurred higher up will have lost its force and what water remains can sometimes sink into the ground sufficiently to support vegetation for years to come.

Vegetation that is typical of mountain terrain includes *Moringa peregrina* and Wild Caper, *Capparis* sp. The capers are particularly attractive as they grow on cliffs in vivid green clumps dotted with large white flowers. However, they flower at night and the flowers fade rapidly after sun-up so they can only be seen at their best in the early morning.

Acacia tortilis raddiana is a common tree of the wadis and the Toothbrush Bush, *Salvadora persica*, although it is a typical representative of wadi vegetation, is scarce. The Toothbrush Bush got its name from the widespread use of its twigs and roots as toothbrushes. The tiny, juicy pink berries are edible and have a pleasant, slightly peppery, flavor. *Balanites aegyptiaca* trees also grow well in this habitat together with the Tamarisk, *Tamarix aphylla*.

The Egyptian Vulture or Pharaoh's Chicken, *Neophron percnopterus*, and the Sand Partridge, *Ammoperdix heyi*, are characteristic birds of the mountains while the wadis provide resting and feeding places for many species of small migrant birds.

Reptiles of the mountains include rock-dwelling lizards such as the Fan-footed Gecko, *Ptyodactylus hasselquistii*, the Spiny Agama, *Agama spinosa*, and Jan's Cliff Racer, *Coluber rhoderhachis*. In the wadi bottoms the Horned Viper, *Cerastes cerastes*, is common. The latter has a more evil reputation than it really deserves for it is a fairly sluggish snake and will often bite as a means of defense without delivering any venom.

The endangered Nubian Ibex, *Capra nubiana*, is king of the mountains but must descend to a wadi water source at least once ever 24 hours to drink. In the wadis Rüppell's Sand Fox, *Vulpes rueppelli*, is a common carnivore and the Caracal, *Caracal caracal*, is als found. The Caracal, in common with most large felines, is under severe pressure.

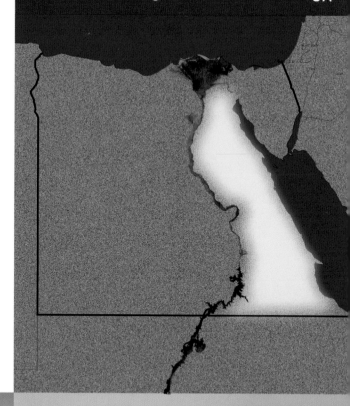

> **This desert is dominated by its spine of rugged mountains seamed with wadis that support the richest assemblage of flora and fauna in Egypt.**

Egyptian Vulture (Pharaoh's Chicken), *Neophron percnopterus:* The juvenile of this small vulture is dark in color, becoming gradually paler until it is fully adult. Less gregarious than other species of vultures it is almost silent. Like all carrion feeders, it is able to detect a carcass from a great distance but due to its small size it is low in the pecking order.

Crowned Sandgrouse, *Pterocles coronatus:* The Crowned Sandgrouse undertakes daily journeys of up to 60km and back to obtain water. When nesting, the bird will get into the available water and soak its breast feathers. When it returns to the nest the chicks drink the water from the feathers. The diet is mainly vegetarian and the 2–3 eggs are incubated by both parents.

Dorcas Gazelle, *Gazella dorcas:* For centuries Arab poets have written about the beauty and grace of gazelles and these slender animals are indeed beautiful. They are, however, less delicate than they seem and can survive in very harsh desert terrain, gaining their fluid from the vegetation they eat and drinking when water is available. Sadly, they are constantly at risk from illegal hunting.

Nubian Ibex, *Capra nubiana:* The handsome, bearded male Ibex crowned with powerful, backswept horns is truly King of the Mountains. These wild relatives of the domestic goat are supremely adapted to their mountain habitat. Unfortunately, they must come down to water every day to drink; at waterholes they are most vulnerable and are not helped by their remarkable agility on the steep mountainsides.

The Horned Viper, *Cerastes cerastes:* The name of this widespread snake of Egyptian deserts can be confusing as not all individuals have the horns, indeed, horned and hornless individuals are often found in the same brood. They hide in the sand with only the eyes showing and wait for their prey. The viper's venom is haemotoxic and prevents the prey's blood from coagulating.

Acacia Tree, *Acacia tortilis raddiana:* A large, drought-resistant tree that is an important component of wadi ecosystems. The creamy-white flowers are in small spherical heads; the twisted pods are edible. The Bedouins shake the leaves from these trees to feed livestock and many animals depend on them for food. Shrikes sometimes use them as 'larders' by spearing prey on the long thorns.

Mangrove, *Avicennia marina*, swamps occur at several localities along the coastline of the Red Sea becoming more frequent and extensive, with larger trees the further south they are. The most northerly stand of mangroves in the Red Sea is found about 26km north of Hurghada at El Gouna. The most extensive stands are found between Bir Shalatin and Halayib, where uninterrupted mangrove forests extend for several kilometers fringing the coastline. South of latitude 23° N another species of Mangrove, *Rhizophora mucronata*, begins to appear but it never becomes as abundant as *Avicennia marina* within Egyptian boundaries.

The mangrove grows as a shrub or small tree to 1 – 3m high. It is uniquely suited to the severe, saline, oxygen-depleted habitat in which it grows and has evolved several strategies to cope. It is usually surrounded by erect stem-like growths called *pneumathodia* that arise from the roots and are thought to provide oxygen for them. The seeds germinate while still on the plant and send out embryonic roots, thus avoiding the necessity of germinating in the extremely saline soil and gaining oxygen at the most important time of germination. A third adaptation is the plant's ability to absorb saline water and excrete the salt on the leaves, which become covered with salt crystals.

The mangroves are vital components of the coastal ecosystem and contribute significantly to the health of the environment as well as providing spawning grounds and havens for many commercially important species of fish and crustaceans.

A number of birds breed in this habitat among them the Striated Heron, *Ardeola striata*, the Spoonbill, *Platylaea leucorodia*, Reef Heron, *Egretta gularis*, and occasionally the Osprey, *Pandion haliaetus*, although the Osprey more often nests on the ground.

Other salt marsh vegetation types

are not particularly common along the coasts of the Red Sea and the Gulf of Suez. Those at El Ain El Sukhna and the deltas of Wadi El Gemal and Wadi El Diib constitute the most significant salt marshes of the Egyptian Red Sea littoral.

Wadi El Gemal runs into the Red Sea about 30km south of Mersa Alam. Close to the shore there is a flowing freshwater spring; the water from which has blended with seawater to form a low-salinity marsh covering approximately 500m². Round the spring there is marsh vegetation of reeds, *Phragmites australis* and *Juncus* spp. Slightly upstream, Tamarisk trees are abundant together with other salt-tolerant plants such as fleshy-leaved *Zygophyllum* spp., which form spreading or cushion-like ground cover.

The Cape Hare, *Lepus capensis*, and the Lesser Egyptian Gerbil, *Gerbillus gerbillus*, are both found here as well as Dorcas Gazelle *Gazella dorcas*. The Semaphore Gecko, *Pristurus flavipunctatus*, is common in coastal Tamarisk thickets. However, it does not appear that any animals are specific to this type of habitat

Intertidal zones,

where the sea and the shore meet and overlap, form valuable habitats for shoreline creatures and often harbor a fascinating variety of shallow-water life forms. These include animals that are well suited to living both underwater and out of water entirely. Often, at low tide, there are tidal pools in which creatures can survive very well until the tide rises and covers the zone again.

Some species of crustaceans, such as shrimps and crabs, and other invertebrates are adapted to this particular lifestyle. Barnacles are among the best adapted of the crustaceans although some species are more tolerant of heat and desiccation than others. The barnacle has been described as "a crustacean, which stands on its head and kicks food into its mouth with its hind legs." Occasionally, a fish gets stranded in a tidal pool and is at risk of becoming easy prey for a hungry sea bird. On stony beaches smaller invertebrates are able to hide under rocks for protection from predators.

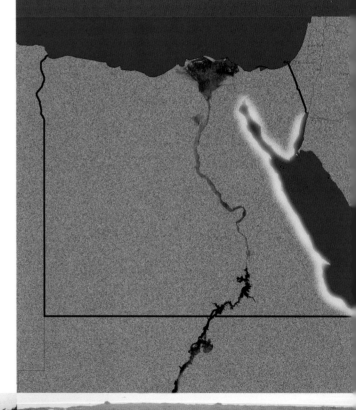

The mangroves are vital components of the coastal flora and contribute significantly to the health of the environment.

10

Upside-down Jellyfish, *Cassiopea* sp: Unlike the familiar translucent, umbrella-shaped pelagic forms of jellyfish, this supine animal lies on its back on the seabed with tentacles and mouth uppermost, to catch passing food. It is seen here in shallow water but can also be found in water as deep as 10m. Its sting is most severe during the breeding season, from April to August.

Ghost Crab, *Ocypode* sp: There are often small mounds built by Ghost Crabs on sandy shores to lure females towards their burrows, which are about 50cm away from the mounds. The crabs then coax the approaching females into the burrows by waving their large claws. These nocturnal animals scavenge along the tide line looking rather ghostly with their eyes carried on long stalks.

Land Hermit crab, Family Coenobitidae: The supreme scavengers of the Red Sea shore, these crabs have gill chambers, which enable them to remain out of water for long periods. At night, they often join forces with Ghost Crabs and small 'armies' of the little creatures move along the shore eating dead fish and whatever other food their sense of smell guides them to.

Sooty Gull, *Larus hemprichii*: This gull is a resident breeder along the Red Sea littoral and nests on the ground, sometimes in the protection of halophytic vegetation such as Suaeda sp. Its diet consists of fish and crustaceans that are sometimes stolen from other birds, as it is rather piratical in its habits. It also steals the eggs and young of other birds.

Reef Heron, *Egretta gularis*: In two months this slightly comic chick will be ready to leave the nest and spend much of its life by the sea. The adult bird sports two long plumes on the head during the breeding season. The Reef Herons are colonial nesters often in Mangroves, which are important to the species. The varied diet includes fish and crustaceans.

Spoonbill, *Platalea leucorodia*: The broad, spoon-shaped bill that gives this large wader its name is used to sift food from seawater. The bird holds the bill vertically and moves it back and forth to capture its crustacean prey. A distinct subspecies is recognized along the Red Sea coast where it nests mainly in Mangroves. The Spoonbill is well represented in Ancient Egyptian art.

Red Sea Islands

There are over 40 islands in the Egyptian Red Sea. That all of them are uninhabitedit and lack terrestrial predators makes them safe havens for nesting sea turtles and a number of sea and shore birds. As the islands are extremely vulnerable to man's meddling, 22 of them are protected by the Ministry of State for Environmental Affairs. These are among the most pristine and unspoiled places on earth with their air of tranquil beauty and the silence that is broken only by the cries of birds and the lapping of the sea.

An archipelago at the mouth of the Gulf of Suez consists of more than 22 islands, while at the mouth of the Gulf of Aqaba the two large islands of Tiran and Sanafir are located; among the more important islands south of Hurghada there are the islands of Safaga, Wadi Gimal and the Hamata group, Zabargad (St John's Island) and the much smaller El Akhawain (Brothers) islands. Smaller groups of islands are found off the delta of Wadi Adaldiib and the village of Abu Ramad. The southernmost island is Halayib.

Vegetation on the islands is generally low and sparse, consisting mainly of a few halophytic species. Mangroves, *Avicennia marina*, are found on some of the islands and form habitat not only for nesting birds but also for a variety of crustaceans.

Among the most fascinating of the shoreline creatures are the Land Hermit Crabs, *Coenobita* sp., which have gill chambers that allow them to stay out of water for varying lengths of time. During the day some species live in burrows or rest in shady coastal vegetation. They help to maintain the pristine beaches by cleaning every scrap of organic matter off them during the night so that in the morning the beaches are spotless. These busy little crabs are truly among nature's clean-up squads.

Two species of lizards, the Turkish Gecko, *Hemidactylus turcicus*, and the Small-spotted Lizard, *Mesalina guttulata*, and the Saharan Sand Snake, *Psammophis aegyptius*, have been seen on some of the larger islands. The beaches on a number of the islands form suitable nesting habitat for marine turtles, notably the Hawksbill, *Eretmochelys imbricata*, and the Green Turtle, *Chelonia mydas*. The other three species of turtles that have been reported from the Red Sea have not been found nesting.

Sixteen species of birds are reported to breed on the Red Sea islands including the Brown Booby, *Sula leucogaster*, and the White-eyed Gull, *Larus leucophthalmus*, which is endemic to the Red Sea. It has been estimated that 30% of the world population of the White-eyed Gull breeds on the islands at the mouth of the Gulf of Suez. In spring and autumn numerous migrating birds use the islands as resting places. The islands also host a significant population of breeding Sooty Falcons, *Falco concolor*.

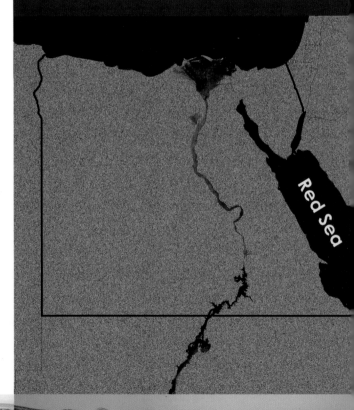

Red Sea islands are safe havens, providing nesting grounds for globally endangered sea turtles and for shore birds.

Red Sea

Bridled Tern, *Sterna anaethetus*: Large numbers of these noisy, colonial nesters breed on the islands of the Red Sea. The nest is a scrape on the ground under dense vegetation cover in which 1–4 eggs are laid; both parents care for the young. Although they are vulnerable on the ground the terns find safely in numbers. They are sometimes called 'sea swallows.'

White-eyed Gull, *Larus leucophthalmus*: This gull is endemic to the Red Sea where about 30% of the world population nests on the islands at the mouth of the Gulf of Suez, preferring open ground near the shore. It has occasionally been found as a vagrant on the Mediterranean coast of Egypt and has been seen as far away as Oman, Iran and Kenya.

Osprey, *Pandion haliaetus*: Egypt has one of the largest breeding populations in the world of this almost pan-geographic bird. Its spectacular dive straight down into the water for its prey can sometimes cause its death by drowning, if it strikes a fish that is too big and fights. Individuals have been seen struggling to carry fishes that were almost too large to manage.

Brown Booby, *Sula leucogaster*: This bird is a pan-tropical, pelagic species that lives exclusively on fish and like the Osprey it dives for its fish prey but with its wings folded. As the webbed feet indicate, it also swims well. It nests on some of the Red Sea islands. Until the chick gets its adult plumage both parents will tend and feed it.

Sooty Falcon, *Falco concolor*: A significant proportion of the world population of Sooty Falcon nests under bushes or in holes in the coral on Red Sea islands although they are also found in the Sahara desert. They nest in the autumn and take advantage of the autumn migration of small passerines to feed their young. At other times they eat bats and insects.

Green Turtle, *Chelonia mydas*: This juvenile, non-breeding Green Turtle belongs to one of the two species that nest in the Red Sea region and is also the only marine turtle that is herbivorous. Nobody knows how or why the females always return to the beach where they were born to lay their eggs or where they go in the many years between hatching and returning.

Coral reefs

Coral reefs are among the most important of all marine habitats and the Red Sea provides ideal environmental conditions for stony corals of which over 200 species are found in this semi-enclosed sea. The shallow shelves bordering the sea ensure sufficient light for calcification to occur and for photosynthesis in the algae on which some polyps feed. The more delicate branching corals thrive in shallow, well-lit water. More massy corals do well in deeper water and are better able to tolerate suspended sediment, which both cuts down available light and tends to clog the little polyps. Corals that are more efficient at cleaning away the sediment do better in areas of relatively high sedimentation.

Symbiotic algae that grow only on live corals produce part of the food the polyps need. Other algae growing on reef faces are food for herbivorous fish and other creatures.

Most stony corals are reef-builders, generally colonial. Each polyp builds a skeleton and the animal sits in a calcareous cup, or theca, that it has secreted. The polyps are connected to each other by an extension of the body above the level of the skeleton. Thus, the colony sits on the surface of the skeleton. In some species, the polyps are widely separated and form branching structures; others are close to each other and have thecal walls in common.

Coral polyps reproduce by means of asexual budding in order to form and enlarge the colony, so colonies can often extend over large areas. The growth rate for some stony corals can be as low as 1cm a year, however, the rate at which coral colonies grow depends on the type of coral, the location and the amount of sunshine they receive. Some corals grow at a rate of 20 – 25cm per year in very good conditions. Others are slow growing at 4 – 5cm per year under very good conditions. Under normal conditions these rates are halved. Breaking off just a few centimeters of coral to take as a souvenir can mean breaking off many years of growth.

Coral reefs provide habitats for many plants and animals. They form an ecological niche in which creatures can live, feed and take refuge from predators. Crustaceans, worms, starfish, and fish all benefit from the coral reef ecosystem.

Called sea grasses

Called sea grasses because they grow in small 'lawns' or 'meadows' and for the long grass-like leaves of many species, these aquatic plants are more closely related to the pondweeds than to the huge family of grasses. Sea grass beds occur on the shallow coastal shelves of the Red Sea and contain eleven of the limited number of species known worldwide. Due to the relative lack of suitable shallow, sedimentary habitat, the number and size of these beds is limited. However, the ecological importance of sea grasses may be comparable to that of the reefs as they are among the richest and most productive of marine ecosystems.

In the Gulf of Aqaba, 49 species of invertebrates were found living in the sea grass beds, of which about 70% were mollusks. About 9% of the species living in these beds were found in no other habitat. Sea grass beds are important providers of food, shelter and protection for the juveniles of various species of commercially important fish and crustaceans and are the only source of food for the Green Turtle, *Chelonia mydas*, and the Dugong, *Dugong dugon*.

It appears that the diet of this large marine mammal consists entirely and solely of one species of sea grass, namely *Halodule uninervis*. It pulls out the grass, using its flippers and makes it into several stacks; it then eats the stacks in more or less serial order.

Offshore waters:

Corals and sea grass beds are found in the shallower waters of the Red Sea but the deeper waters are also home to a great diversity of fish that feed on plankton, invertebrates or each other. Among these, the largest and most well known are the sharks of which several species are found in this zone. Cetaceans are also not uncommon in Egyptian waters and include Risso's Dolphin, *Grampus griseus*, and Bryde's Whale, *Balaenoptera edeni*.

The Red Sea provides ideal environmental conditions for corals of which over 200 species are found in this semi-enclosed sea.

Red Sea

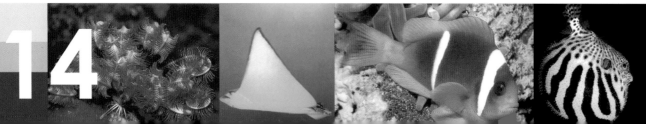

ea Fan, _Acabaria splendens_: The sea fans are colonial corals upported by a horny fan-like structure. In contrast, the reef-building corals build a solid calcareous structure. This is a typical deep water coral of Red Sea reefs and mostly grows in caves or under overhangs. The flower-like, white organs are the tentacles and are used to trap the plankton on which the polyps feed.

Dugong, _Dugong dugon_: These gentle, harmless mammals are as completely aquatic as the whales and dolphins but remain in shallow water. They can grow to over 3m and weigh more than 400kg. They are widespread in suitable habitats in the Red Sea but are very endangered and are uncommon. They are strictly herbivorous and their diet is restricted to the sea grass, Halodule uninervis.

Sohal Surgeonfish, _Acanthurus sohal_: This beautiful and colorful fish is a very aggressive territorial species that is characteristic of coral reef habitats. It gets its name 'surgeonfish' from the razor-sharp, hinged spine that folds into a groove on each side of the peduncle. It can slash other fishes, or a human who tries to handle it, with a side sweep of its tail.

Crown Butterflyfish, _Chaetodon paucifasciatus_: The family of Butterflyfishes is represented in the Red Sea by 14 species of which seven are endemic to the region; nearly all of them are brightly colored. The Crown Butterflyfishes are often seen in pairs or small groups and are generally diurnal in habit. They feed on the polyps of Sea Fans and stony corals, small crustaceans and algae.

Silky Shark, _Carcharhinus falciformis_: Although they are carnivorous, not all sharks are vicious and indiscriminate killers. Sharks have cartilaginous skeletons, which are lighter than bone; they also have huge oily livers and these two factors assist their buoyancy. They are very fast swimmers and are often accompanied by Pilotfishes or Remoras. Over fishing is having a serious negative impact on shark populations worldwide.

Breastspot Cleaner Wrasse, _Labroides pectoralis_: This little fish sets up a cleaning station on the reef and 'clients' come to have troublesome parasites such as sealice and copepods removed. The parasites often attach themselves between the gills or teeth of the host so the fish opens its mouth and gill cavities while being cleaned. Here a Great Moray, _Gymnothorax javanicus_, is being tended.

Mountains and Wadis of South Sinai

The spectacular mountains and wadis of South Sinai take up approximately one-third of the peninsula. At the heart of these mountains is the St Katherine Protectorate in which the highest peaks in Egypt are found. The highest mountain is Gebel Katherina (2641m). The mountains are seamed with wadis that drain eastward to the Gulf of Aqaba or west to the Sahl El Qa and the Gulf of Suez. Although rainfall averages just 62mm annually, it occasionally exceeds 300mm on the highest peaks where it falls principally as snow. It is the only place in Egypt where there is snow in the winter and the temperature can fall to as low as -10°C.

As with other mountain terrain in Egypt, flash floods often denude the narrow wadi bottoms of vegetation. Despite this, the relative abundance of precipitation and a number of springs in the wadis support a rich diversity of plant and animal life including more than 50% of all the plants that are endemic to Egypt. Among the endemics is the endangered Sinai Rose, *Rosa arabica*. A plant that is rare in Sinai but is not endemic is *Rubus sanctus*; traditionally the Burning Bush of the Bible.

The Sinai Rosefinch, *Carpodacus synoicus*, which in spite of its name has its main area of distribution in Central Asia, and Tristram's Grackle, *Onycognathus tristramii*, are found, in Egypt, only in this region. The Lammergeier, *Gypaetus barbatus*, is becoming increasingly rare throughout its world range but probably breeds in very small numbers here.

The Ornate Spiny-tailed Lizard, *Uromastyx ornata*, which inhabits rocky slopes and mountains, is a smaller and more brightly colored relative of the Dhab or Egyptian Spiny-tailed Lizard, *Uromastyx aegyptia*, an inhabitant of sandy plains and wadis. The Sinai Banded Snake, *Coluber sinai*, and Hoogstraal's Cat Snake, *Telescopus hoogstraali*, are endemic to Sinai. Also here, is the extremely poisonous Palestine Mole Viper, *Atractaspis microlepidota*, which is undoubtedly the most dangerous snake in the region and is not found elsewhere in Egypt.

The Garden Dormouse, *Eliomys quercinus*, is an attractive member of the local fauna and is sometimes called the Bandit in reference to the black 'mask' over the eyes. This attractive little dormouse belies its appearance by being rather aggressive and is well prepared to defend itself with its sharp teeth. Although Blanford's Fox, *Vulpes cana*, has been known from further east (Pakistan and Iran among other countries) for a long time, this beautiful, small, bushy-tailed fox has only been known to be in the Sinai since the early 1980s. A small population of the Wolf, *Canis lupus*, has recently been documented in the region. The very rare and endangered Sinai Leopard, *Panthera pardus jarvisi*, may still be extant in very small numbers.

As well as its rich fauna and flora, South Sinai has a wealth of cultural and religious history including the site of St Katherine's Monastery, which has been occupied by Christians since at least the early fourth century. It has been suggested that Wadi Feiran may have been the home of the Amalekites of early Biblical times.

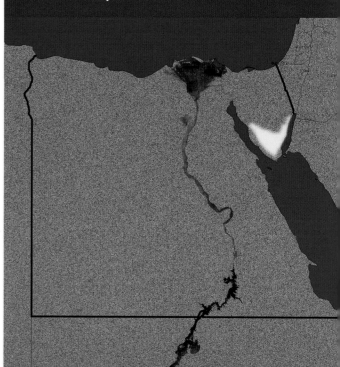

The spectacular mountains and wadis of South Sinai take up approximately one-third of the entire Sinai peninsula.

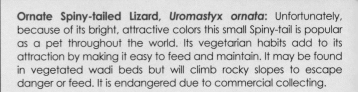

Sinai Rosefinch, *Carpodacus synoicus*: Another case of difference between the unassuming, gray-brown female and the vividly colored male. Both have the typical stout beaks of seedeaters. The bright colors of the male do not prevent it from 'vanishing' on the rocky slopes where it lives. A somewhat surprising bird to find in South Sinai as its main area of distribution is Central Asia.

Hume's Tawny Owl, *Strix butleri*: A fairly rare owl, or perhaps just rarely seen, so its range may be more extensive than previously realized. It has just recently been found to be widespread in the coastal desert of Sinai. This is a very territorial owl and has been known to attack a tape recorder that was playing the call of a different individual.

Ornate Spiny-tailed Lizard, *Uromastyx ornata*: Unfortunately, because of its bright, attractive colors this small Spiny-tail is popular as a pet throughout the world. Its vegetarian habits add to its attraction by making it easy to feed and maintain. It may be found in vegetated wadi beds but will climb rocky slopes to escape danger or feed. It is endangered due to commercial collecting.

Burton's Carpet Viper, *Echis coloratus*: This extremely dangerous snake may be found in vegetated rocky wadis and occasionally climbs on trees. The coloration of the Carpet Viper is variable although the pattern never changes. Snakes of the genus *Echis* are responsible for more snakebite fatalities than all other snakes in the world. Nine species of potentially dangerous venomous snakes are found in Egypt.

Hyrax, *Procavia capensis*: This small, diurnal herbivore is hunted for food. The forefeet have four short toes with hoof-like extremities; the hind feet have three. The upper incisors of this relative of the elephant are curved and tusk-like. Scattered tactile bristles in the fur assist it to navigate the narrow rock crevices where it lives. The only mammal in Egypt to post sentries.

Thistle, *Onopordum* sp: A beautiful example of the many spiny thistles in the Compositae family, which includes lettuce and the herb tarragon. The characteristic that distinguishes the Compositae from all other plant families is that what looks like a single flower is actually a varying number of tiny flowers called florets forming a single head or capitulum.

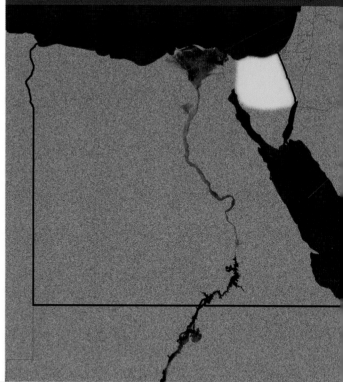

Central and North Sinai

The Central Plateaus of Sinai: The high limestone plateau of Gabal El Igma (1620m) in Central Sinai forms the southern end of the northward dipping El Tih Plateau. The northward limit of El Tih is marked by a series of hills ranging from 370m to 1094m in height including Gebel El-Maghara, which is one of the proposed new Protected Areas. Numerous dendritic wadis drain the plateaus northwards into the lower areas of North Sinai and the great Wadi El Arish, which flows into the northern plain. These wadis often support a rich and diverse flora, one of the dominant species being White Wormwood, *Artemisia herba-alba*, which is used by the Bedouins to flavor tea and for relieving stomach upsets.

A typical reptile of the plateaus is the brightly hued Starred Agama, *Laudakia stellio*. The rare False Horned Viper, *Pseudocerastes persicus*, is also found in the region.

The Golden Eagle, *Aquila chrysaetos*, is nowhere common but has been reported as a resident breeding bird of this zone. The Barbary Partridge, *Alectoris barbara*, also breeds here.

Among the mammals, the Indian Crested Porcupine, *Hystrix indica*, which is fairly common in the Hijaz and Asir of Saudi Arabia, has been reported from this area in recent years. The Marbled Polecat, *Vormela peregusna*, has also been recently discovered in the region. The Barbastelle, *Barbastella barbastellus*, a small Vespertilionid bat, has not been recorded from any other region in Egypt.

The Mediterranean **coastal desert** of Sinai is formed of wide sandy plains that slope towards the Mediterranean. It receives less rain than the Western Desert Mediterranean Coastal Zone and is therefore more sparsely vegetated. While this area is generally rather featureless, eolian sand dunes of 10 to 80m high are common. The broad outwash of Wadi El Arish, fed by numerous tributaries, was historically known for its agriculture and olive and palm groves are still found here.

Among the more interesting resident birds found here is the Syrian Woodpecker, *Dendrocopus syriacus*, the Serin, *Serinus serinus*, and Spotted Flycatcher, *Muscicapa striata*, which are found nowhere else in Egypt. The Houbara Bustard, *Chlamydotis undulata*, is also a resident together with the Cream-colored Courser, *Cursorius cursor*. During the spring and autumn migrations, the Mediterranean Coastal Desert of Sinai receives vast populations of Palearctic migrant birds.

This zone is one of the last places where the increasingly rare and endangered Egyptian Tortoise, *Testudo kleinmanni*, listed in the 2000 IUCN Red List of Threatened Animals, is still found. In the Zaranik Protected Area a project for the conservation of this tortoise is currently underway.

Other reptiles of this coastal desert are the Nidua Lizard, *Acanthodactylus scutellatus*, Desert Monitor, *Varanus griseus*, and the Common Chameleon, *Chamaeleo chamaeleon*. The presence of the Syrian Black Snake, *Coluber jugularis*, in the area has been questioned in the past but it is well known to the Bedouins. The endangered Green Turtle, *Chelonia mydas*, and Loggerhead Turtle, *Caretta caretta*, nest sporadically on the sandy Mediterranean shore.

About twenty species of mammals are reported from this zone among them the Cape Hare, *Lepus capensis*, Indian Crested Porcupine, *Hystrix indica*, The Sand Cat, *Felis margarita*, Fennec Fox, *Vulpes zerda*, and Lesser Jerboa, *Jaculus jaculus*.

One of Egypt's most scenic eco-zones, with an exceptional variety of birds; terrestrial habitats harbor several globally threatened species.

18

Snipe, *Gallinago gallinago*: This cryptically colored bird is readily identified by its long bill and sturdy build. In its preferred habitat of fairly thick vegetation it can become almost invisible. It breeds in summer in wet swamps or bogs in northern Europe, but prefers drier regions in the winter and occurs in small numbers among the many migrant birds to be seen in North Sinai.

European Kingfisher, *Alcedo atthis*: One of the most colorful birds of the region, the Kingfisher is a migrant in Egypt, where it is commonly seen on canals and waterways. It is inclined to be solitary and catches its fish prey by swooping from a perch into the water. In flight, the short tail and fairly stocky build give it an almost cigar-shaped appearance.

Sand Cat, *Felis margarita*: A beautiful small cat with soft dense fur and thick mats of long wavy hair that cover the palms and soles and enable this cat to negotiate soft sandy terrain with ease. The very low-set ears may be an adaptation that allows it to flatten itself as much as possible when stalking its small mammal prey in scant cover

Savigny's Agama, *Trapelus savignii*: A distinctive lizard that is restricted in range to North Sinai and Southern Palestine. It is a diurnal species that is well adapted to its habitat of sandy areas or, less commonly, gravel plains and may climb on desert shrubs in very hot weather. The coloration is generally dull but is enlivened by its blue throat and violet sides.

Egyptian Tortoise, *Testudo kleinmanni*: A small, high-domed, vegetarian tortoise that is extremely endangered as, like other small tortoises, it is popular with the pet trade. It is largely endemic to Libya and Egypt and in Egypt its range is restricted to the Mediterranean coastal deserts. Fortunately, a small population is still extant in North Sinai and is currently the subject of conservation efforts.

False Horned viper, *Pseudocerastes persicus*: This rather stoutly built snake may be differentiated from the Horned Viper by its heavier build and the tubercles over each eye, which are shorter and broader than the 'horns' of the Horned Viper. The coloration is also less well defined. This species is found, in Egypt, only in Sinai but is not common anywhere within its range.

The lakes and wetlands of the Mediterranean Delta coast form an important eco-zone especially for migrating and wintering water birds.

Lake Maryut, just south of Alexandria, has no direct connection to the sea and lies at 2.8m below sea level. Agricultural drainage water enters the lake through canals causing the water level to rise and to maintain the level, excess water is pumped out into the sea. To the west of the lake is a large saltmarsh that was formerly part of the lake but was separated from it when the railway line was constructed in 1858.

East of Lake Maryut is Lake Idku, the northern shore of which is covered with sand dunes except for a single gap that connects it to the sea. The salinity of this lake is relatively high but where agricultural water drains into it in its southern part the water is only slightly brackish. There are many small islands in Lake Idku and an extensive marsh has developed where the drainage canals enter.

Lake Burullus is located slightly east of the Rosetta branch of the Nile and is extremely shallow, varying from 0.75m to 1m in depth. The eastern portion of this rather elongated lake is the shallowest and there are about 50 small islands scattered throughout its area. The sandbar that separates the lake from the sea varies in width from a few hundred meters in the east to about 5km at the western end. The only connection between the lake and the sea is at the northeast corner and here the water is most saline. The salinity decreases to the south and the water is fresh near the canals and drains that enter the lake. Commercial salt production and fish farming are carried on to the south of the lake where there are salt marshes.

Lake Manzala, east of Damietta, is the largest of the Delta lakes and has most connections with the sea. The salinity is highest in the northwest and lowest near the drain and canal inflows on the south and east. The rest of the lake is brackish. There are over 1000 islands scattered throughout the lake and fish farms take up large areas of its northwest.

The shallowest of the lakes is Lake Mallaha/Bur Fuad. It is only 10 – 20cm deep with a soft muddy bottom and receives no Nile water but is connected to the sea. There are extensive areas of *sabkha* round it.

The extremely saline Lake Bardawil is an important feature of the north coast of Sinai and stretches along much of its length. The lake is separated from the Mediterranean by a low sandbar that is between 100m and 1km wide and is often covered by seawater. The sandy bottom of this shallow lake (0.5 – 3.0m) is covered by patches of the ditch grass, *Ruppia spiralis* and there is a number of islands. Lake Bardawil is important for its fishery of up to 2500 tonnes annually, mostly of such high-value fish as Gilthead, *Sparus auratus*, and Mullet, *Mugil* sp. In the immediate vicinity of the lake Little Tern, *Sterna albifrons*, and Kentish Plover, *Charadrius alexandrinus*, are found in internationally important numbers.

Most of the lakes support extensive reed swamps of *Typha* and *Phragmites* and areas of halophytic vegetation. Lake Manzala contains submerged aquatic plants such as *Najas armata* and the Pondweed, *Potamogeton pectinatus*.

Many thousands of birds winter on these lakes and include Gulls (*Larus minutus* and *L. ridibundus* among others), Greater Flamingo, *Phoenicopterus ruber*, and White-breasted Cormorant, *Phalacrocorax carbo*. Lake Manzala is the most important wetland in Egypt for wintering waterbirds and for some breeding species is one of the most important areas in the Western Palearctic.

The Green Toad, *Bufo viridis*, is found in somewhat brackish water, while *Bufo kassasii* is a freshwater species. Tessellated Water Snake, *Natrix tessellata*, has been recorded in freshwater marshes; Bridled Skink, *Mabuya vittata*, occurs round freshwater and brackish water marshes.

Swamp Cat, *Felis chaus*, is known to occur in *Phragmites* and *Typha* reed swamps and other shore vegetation at some of the lakes.

The lakes and wetlands that fringe the Mediterranean coast of the Nile Delta and Sinai cover an area that totals at least 280,000 hectares.

Mediteranean Sea

Whiskered Tern, *Chlidonias hybrida*: A major part of the world population of these terns is found on Lakes Manzala and Burullus where it is a winter visitor. It is believed that it may have started breeding in the wetlands of northern Egypt in recent years. This is a marsh tern, is insectivorous and is smaller and darker than most of the sea terns.

Pied Kingfisher, *Ceryle rudis*: This striking, large kingfisher has the sexes slightly different; the male has two black bands on the chest, the female only one. Although mainly resident, it may disperse somewhat in the winter. It appears to prefer fresh water and its characteristic method of fishing is by hovering several meters above the water, then plummeting down to catch its prey.

Spur-winged Plover, *Vanellus spinosus*: The distinctive coloration of this bird renders it easily noticeable in its preferred open habitat near fresh or brackish water. It feeds mainly on insects, mollusks, worms, crustaceans and vegetable matter. Both parents incubate the 2–4 eggs in a nest on the ground and tend the young.

Squacco Heron, *Ardeola ralloides*: This is one of the smallest herons in the region and is one of the 35 species of birds that breed in the vicinity of Lake Manzala; it is a colonial nester in thickets, trees or reeds. The diet is mainly fish, amphibians, small mammals, birds, and insects. Both parents rear the 3–6 young and feed them by regurgitation.

Kassas's Toad, *Bufo kassasii*: A newly described species that is abundant in Delta wetlands. It is rather small in size with a maximum recorded length of 4cm. The male makes a distinctive rattle-like call. This toad inhabits flooded swamps and rice fields and is known in Egypt only from the Nile Valley south to Luxor. It is closely related to several Afrotropical species.

Bulrush, *Typha domingensis*: This tall reed-like plant with long linear leaves grows up to 2m and is common in ditches and marshy places. The male and female flowers are on the same stem separated by a naked space; the male flowers are above. The 'ark of bulrushes' in which the daughter of Pharaoh found the baby Moses was actually made of Papyrus reeds.

The Nile Valley and Delta

Herodotus described Egypt as 'the gift if the Nile' and for millennia the Nile Valley and the Delta *was* Egypt. The harsh deserts that form most of modern Egypt were not considered.

Together the river and its delta form a typical river oasis. From Lake Nasser in the south to the apex of the Delta roughly at Cairo in the north, the Nile Valley averages 10km in width. The Delta is 166km from its apex to the Mediterranean coast and is 250km wide.

Today, after at least 7,000 years of human activity, this river oasis is essentially a man-made ecosystem and the area is extensively cultivated. The trees that grow in the cities are largely introduced, many of them beautiful ornamentals such as the pink-flowered *Cassia nodosa*, the Flame Tree, *Delonix regia*, and *Bauhinia variegata* among others. The fertile soil of the Nile Valley and the Delta nurtures an enormous variety of fruits and vegetables that originated far from Egypt. Plants that do well in cooler weather are grown during the winter months while others thrive in the warm summer temperatures. Native plants also thrive in this habitat, which is home to six species that are endemic to this zone and three endemics that are found in other eco-zones of Egypt as well.

Animals that inhabit the region are either commensal or able to tolerate human activities. The Nile Rat, *Arvicanthis niloticus*, is common in the region together with the Long-eared Hedgehog, *Hemiechinus auritus*, the Wildcat, *Felis sylvestris*, and the Weasel, *Mustela nivalis*, which is found in Cairo and Alexandria. Among the reptiles that inhabit this eco-zone are the African Beauty Snake, *Psammophis sibilans*, Tessellated Water Snake, *Natrix tessellata*, which is common in streams and irrigation canals of the Delta and the Ocellated Skink, *Chalcides ocellatus*. Several amphibian species are also found in the region, most commonly the Square-marked Toad, *Bufo regularis*, which can be heard calling in urban gardens even in Central Cairo. .

The abundance of available food and water attracts many migrating birds that winter in the area, augmenting the resident population of about 66 breeding species among which are the Senegal Coucal, *Centropus senegalensis*, and the Senegal Thick-knee, *Burhinus senegalensis*, the distinctive call of which can be heard in Cairo during the night.

Lake Nasser is the name of the northern portion of the reservoir that formed after the Aswan High Dam was built. Although Lake Nasser covers an area of 5248km^2, its surface area fluctuates according to the volume of the annual Nile flood. Numerous dendritic extensions of the lake are the flooded lower portions of wadis that drain into the Nile Valley. These extensions are known as *khors* and some of them extend for many kilometers into the desert. The shores and islands of this lake often support dense vegetation.

While Lake Nasser does not appear to have attracted migratory water birds in the past, it now seems be becoming increasingly important as a wintering area for waterbirds, particularly Tufted Duck, *Aythya fuligula*. The lake also provides the only known breeding habitat for the Egyptian Goose, *Alopochen aegyptiacus*, in Egypt.

The reptiles of this zone include the Nile Crocodile, *Crocodylus niloticus*, the Nile Monitor, *Varanus niloticus*, and the Nile Soft-shell Turtle, *Trionyx triunguis*, which is also restricted to this habitat. The dog-like Jackal, *Canis aureus*, is found here, as is the Sand Cat, *Felis margarita*.

Today, after at least 7,000 years of human activity, this river oasis is essentially a man-made ecosystem.

22

Palm Dove, *Streptopelia senegalensis*: A familiar bird of the Nile Valley that is sometimes called the Laughing Dove. Like other doves, this common bird of Africa and the Middle East is extending its range. Nests are on trees, bushes or houses but the Palm Dove seems to be a rather poor builder and eggs often fall through holes in the carelessly constructed nest.

Senegal Thick-knee, *Burhinus senegalensis*: This large bird is common in cities like Cairo where it nests on roofs and can often be heard calling in the night but is rarely seen. It is seldom found far from water and sometimes nests on river sandbanks. These carnivorous birds are excellent parents and both participate in incubating the eggs and rearing the (usually) two chicks.

Nile Soft-shelled Turtle, *Trionyx triunguis*: The only soft-shelled turtles found in Africa, this species can grow to 90cm long and 45kg in weight. They were formerly common in the Nile but are now restricted to Lake Nasser. These turtles are said to be vicious. Some wander down the Nile into the sea and they have been seen on the Mediterranean coast of Sinai.

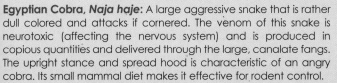

Egyptian Cobra, *Naja haje*: A large aggressive snake that is rather dull colored and attacks if cornered. The venom of this snake is neurotoxic (affecting the nervous system) and is produced in copious quantities and delivered through the large, canalate fangs. The upright stance and spread hood is characteristic of an angry cobra. Its small mammal diet makes it effective for rodent control.

Nile Crocodile, *Crocodylus niloticus*: This typical representative of the true crocodiles, grows to about 4.5m and is often seen basking on sandbars in Lake Nasser. Crocodiles have powerful jaws and teeth and laterally compressed tails bearing dorsal crests of strong erect scales. In summer, the female lays from 20–30 eggs, covering them thoroughly and defending the nest vigorously until the hatchlings emerge.

Red Fox, *Vulpes vulpes*: A very widespread fox with an almost pan-geographic range in several subspecies. This supremely adaptable fox may be distinguished from all other species by the white tip to the tail and black back to the ears. Usually subsists on small birds, reptiles and mammals but also scavenge trash heaps and appears to be fond of fruit, particularly watermelons.

Gebel Uweinat and Gilf Kebir

Gebel Uweinat is a sandstone and granite massif lying on the southwest corner of Egypt. At 1907m, it represents the highest point of the Western Desert and covers an area of 1500km². Rainfall is extremely sparse and unpredictable here, occurring only about once every ten years, however, when rain does fall it fills rock basins that are found in the narrow winding gorges that seam the massif. The only vegetation that occurs in the Egyptian section of this mountain is found in Karkur Talh.

The sandstone plateau of Gilf Kebir lies to the north of Gebel Uweinat and is much larger in area. Its rocky surface, which slopes southeastward from 1000m to 600m, is partially covered by sand sheets. The Great Sand Sea to the north is gradually encroaching on this plateau and the slowly moving dune systems are already creeping into the wadis and up the rocky slopes. The plateau is dissected by wadis of which the most prominent are Wadi Talh, Wadi Abd El Malik and Wadi Hamra, so called because the sand there is red ('Hamra' [*ahmar*] means 'red' in Arabic).

Owing to the extreme aridity of the area plants and animals are scarce although the extensive rock art in the wadis of Gebel Uweinat and, to a lesser extent Gilf Kebir, attest to an earlier, wetter period with ostriches, giraffe, gazelle and many cattle.

Despite the extreme nature of the climate, some wadis do support trees of *Acacia tortilis raddiana* and *Maerua crassifolia*. In some of the larger wadis *Zilla spinosa* grows and flowers when conditions allow, together with a few of the hardier species of grasses such as *Panicum turgidum*. The Bitter or Desert Melon, *Citrullus colocynthis*, is also found in this zone. On the very rare occasions when there is a little rain the area briefly becomes green as opportunist plants burst forth, set seed and die within the space of time it takes for the damp sand to dry out again. Gebel Uweinat is said to boast a flora of at least 55 species.

Little is known of the reptiles of this region but at least one species, the Egyptian Gecko, *Tarentola annularis*, is found here together with its insect food. It is always a surprise to people unfamiliar with the desert that in the most arid and apparently lifeless areas, nighttime brings out thousands of insects. Insectivorous birds such as the White-crowned Black Wheatear, *Oenanthe leucopyga*, do well in this zone. Other small birds have been reported from these desolate areas, including the Desert Lark, *Ammomanes deserti*, and, rather surprisingly, the House Bunting, *Emberiza striolata*, which is mainly a seedeater but will also eat insects.

The leaves and fruits of the plants provide food for a small population of the highly endangered Barbary Sheep, *Ammotragus lervia*. Although these hardy animals survive on the moisture they get from their plant food, they do drink when water is available.

There are many thousands of rock paintings and engravings in the Sahara and Libyan deserts and many are to be seen at Gebel Uweinat in the wadi known as Karkur Talh where over 4,000 have been found. A high proportion of the drawings depict various sorts of cattle. The Goran tribesmen who lived here in the 1920s believed that the artwork was done by Djinns in olden days.

Rainfall is extremely sparse and unpredictable here, occurring only about once every ten years.

White-crowned Black Wheatear, *Oenanthe leucopyga*: This strikingly marked small bird is characteristic of rocky wadis of the Egyptian deserts, often in areas that are devoid of vegetation and except in years of some rainfall may be the only bird seen in the Gebel Uweinat area. Immature males and females lack the white crown. These insectivorous birds are sometimes seen hawking for flies.

Egyptian Gecko, *Tarentola annularis*: A typical lizard of rocky deserts of southern Egypt, this gecko can live in very dry areas obtaining sufficient moisture from its insect food. If the tail is seized by a pursuer, it can break off and is able to grow back again although not as perfectly as the original. The tail is necessary to aid the lizard's balance.

Nidua Lizard, *Acanthodactylus scutellatus*: This lizard is widespread in the sandy deserts of Egypt where its diet consists mainly of small insects, especially ants. It is diurnal in habit but is generally more active in the early morning and late afternoon during the hottest times of the year and in the middle of the day during the winter when the weather is cool.

Barbary sheep, *Ammotragus lervia*: These are hardy and robustly built animals that can withstand severe drought, getting their moisture requirements from plants. A small population of these handsome and extremely endangered wild sheep still survives in Gilf Kebir. They were also widespread in the mountains of the Eastern Desert where they are now confined to a small area near Gebel Elba.

Bitter or Desert Melon, *Citrullus colocynthis*: This relative of the cucumber and melon is common in arid areas. It is prostrate with long trailing stems, branched tendrils and bright yellow flowers. The young fleshy fruits are yellow with dark green stripes and age to pure yellow. The fruit's pulp and seeds are strongly laxative and have been used for medicinal purposes for millennia.

Woody Caper, *Maerua crassifolia*: This interesting and drought resistant plant can grow as a small shrub or as a tree. The wood is extremely hard, often with spines or tubercles; the attractive large white flowers are clusters of long stamens growing a few together on twigs. It has small dark-green leaves and is sometimes heavily grazed, providing food for desert herbivores.

Sands and Sand Dunes of the Western Desert

Although the **Western Desert** is essentially a flat rocky plateau, much of its vast expanse is covered by eolian (wind blown) sand and the Great Sand Sea of Egypt is part of one of the largest sand-covered areas on earth. The Great Sand Sea extends from the Libyan border west of Siwa Oasis in a generally southerly direction touching the oases of Farafra and Dakhla on the east and ending at the Gilf Kebir at its southernmost tip.

Sand dunes, which cover large areas of the Western Desert, have a variety of forms and complexity that depend on the wind regime and sand abundance. In the north, longitudinal dunes known as *seif* (sword) or *irq* predominate, while to the south barchan or crescent-shaped dunes are more common. Some other forms, such as parallel wavy dune complexes are found but are less common. Dunes move at a more or less fixed rate in the direction of the prevailing wind. Thus, the southernmost fingers of the Great Sand Sea are encroaching on the wadis of Gilf Kebir.

Between large longitudinal *seif* dunes there are often inter-dune valleys that can support a wealth of plant and animal life. Mobile dune types are less well supplied with wildlife. Phytogenic mounds that form round such plants as *Nitraria retusa*, *Calligonum comosum* or *Tamarix* spp. add greatly to this habitat's diversity and create niches for animals and birds.

The waterless expanse of this desert is home to an assemblage of animals that are well adapted to living without water and gain their moisture from their food. Many animals have evolved behavioral or morphological features that enable them to survive the extremely hot climate or for locomotion on soft sand. The Lesser Sand Viper, *Cerastes vipera*, which can easily be confused with hornless specimens of the Horned Viper, *Cerastes cerastes*, is only found in sandy habitats. Another denizen of the sands is the Sandfish, *Scincus scincus*, so named because of its habit of 'swimming' through the sand.

A number of birds inhabit the sands especially the Hoopoe Lark, *Alaemon alaudipes*, which is easily distinguished from other larks by the long, slightly curved bill that gives it its name and also by its remarkable display flight.

Mammals of the region include the now extremely rare Slender-horned Gazelle, *Gazella leptoceros*. This animal lives largely on such plants as *Nitraria retusa*, *Cornulaca monacantha* and *Calligonum comosum*. An immensely appealing animal of the sands is the tiny Fennec Fox, *Vulpes zerda*, which may be one of the most well adapted desert carnivores in the world. They dig rather deep burrows so that exposure to heat during the day is reduced to a minimum and appear to be the only desert carnivores that can live entirely without water.

In the southwest of the Great Sand Sea, immediately to the north of Gilf Kebir, the curious phenomenon known as Libyan Desert silica glass is found. The pieces of glass can be pale green or creamy in color, can be clear or opaque and weigh from a few grams to seven or eight kilograms. These beautiful pieces of glass, lying between the sand dunes, are natural formations and studies during most of the twentieth century have failed to reveal their origin. In 1998, it was discovered that a giant lime-green scarab, the centerpiece of King *Tutankhamun's* jeweled, ceremonial pectoral was not, as had previously been thought, made of chalcedony but was Libyan Desert silica glass.

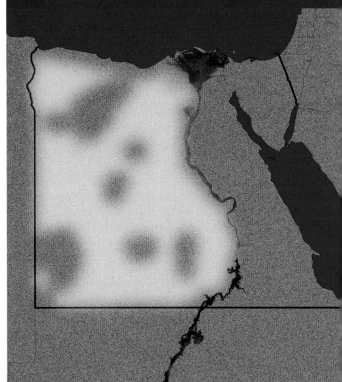

Sand dunes, which cover large areas of the Western Desert, have a variety of forms and complexity that depend on the wind regime and sand abundance.

26

Slender-horned Gazelle, *Gazella leptoceros*: Over hunting has seriously reduced the population of this endangered animal. It is well adapted to soft sandy desert and is active during the cooler parts of the day and possibly at night. In the heat of the day it lies under an Acacia tree or scrapes a pit in the sand to avail of the little shade afforded.

Fennec Fox, *Vulpes zerda*: The huge ears of this nocturnal carnivore may aid heat dissipation as well as assisting the acute hearing. The palms and soles are covered by long soft hair, enabling them to move easily on soft sand. Food consists largely of insects, lizards and rodents; it may be one of the few desert carnivores that are entirely independent of water.

Lesser Sand Viper, *Cerastes vipera*: An exclusively sand dwelling snake that can easily be mistaken for a hornless Horned Viper. However, the habitats of each are different. It apparently feeds largely on lizards and rodents but has been known to take small birds. This snake has the classic broad head and sidewinding locomotion of this family of sand-dwelling vipers.

Audouin's Sand Skink, *Sphenops sepsoides*: This slim, sand skink with very short limbs has the habit of 'swimming' just below the surface of the sand, leaving a characteristic raised, winding track. It lives to a large extent on fossorial (burrowing) insects that it is able to catch under the sand. It is believed to be mainly nocturnal in summer and diurnal in winter.

Saharan Fringe-toed Lizard, *Acanthodactylus longipes*: The long digits of this lizard are fringed with scales, which give it its name. It occupies soft sand dunes where it can move extremely fast in order to evade predators. During the heat of the day it will stand on tiptoe to avoid its body making contact with the hot sand. It subsists mainly on small insects.

Lanner Falcon, *Falco biarmicus*: The population of this beautiful bird of prey is now considerably reduced owing to them being trapped as decoys to catch the more desirable Saker, *Falco cherrug*, and Peregrine, *Falco peregrinus*, falcons for sale to falconers in the Gulf States. Both resident and migratory in Egypt.

Western Desert Depressions and Oases

Between the coastal zone and the Western Desert proper are numerous groves of *Acacia tortilis raddiana*. These groves stretch from the Nile Valley to the border of Libya and can vary in size from a few to several hundred trees of assorted sizes. Acacia trees can live in areas that get 10mm rain or less annually and are apparently able to survive for long periods on the mere memory of moisture. Many ephemeral herbs grow in association with the trees and form an important food source for highly mobile herbivores such as Dorcas Gazelle, *Gazella dorcas*.

There are seven major depressions in the Western Desert, of which the most northerly and by far the largest is the Qattara Depression, which covers an area of 19,500km² and encompasses sabkhas, lakes and salt marshes of 5,800km². At its lowest point this depression is 134m below sea level. This vast depression is very sparsely inhabited and due to the inaccessibility of much of its area, is refuge for otherwise rare species such as the Cheetah, *Acinonyx jubatus*, and the Dorcas Gazelle, *Gazella dorcas*.

Siwa Oasis, which lies to the west of the Qattara Depression, has a long and checkered history. Although there is no evidence that it was known during the Old, Middle or New Kingdoms, it is possible that it was colonized during the Twenty-sixth Dynasty (664 – 525 B.C.). By 331 B.C. when Alexander the Great went there to consult the Oracle, Siwa was known throughout the Mediterranean region.

The earliest name for Siwa was *Sekhet-imit* (the Place of the Palm Trees). It could well be called that today, for this 82km-long, rather narrow depression abounds with palm groves and its dates are famous throughout Egypt. Palm trees, which do well on brackish water, olives and a few vegetables are the only crops grown in Siwa because, although there are many lakes and more than a thousand springs, the water is very saline.

Other major depressions have potable water and have been settled and cultivated for thousands of years. The Fayoum Depression is closest to Cairo and has a history that goes back to the Old Kingdom (2613 – 2181 B.C.) of Ancient Egypt. This depression receives its potable water from the Nile by means of three canals: the Ibrahamiya and Bahr Wahbi canals and the Bahr Yusuf, which is very ancient and may be a natural branch of the Nile. The Fayoum has been known since earliest times for its agriculture. It is also famous for its extraordinary assemblage of fossil animals, among which is a Hyrax, *Megalohyrax*, as big as a pony. Another elephantid called *Arsinotherium* was 2m high at the shoulder and had immense horns on its nose.

Among the characteristic birds of these habitats are the Rufous Bush Robin, *Cercotrichas galactotes*, and the Turtle Dove, *Streptopelia turtur*. Many small migratory species take advantage of these habitats and feed on the mosquitoes for which some of the depressions are notorious.

In the dry *sabkhas* (salt flats) of the depressions and surrounding desert, a few reptile species are found, including the Fringe-toed Lizard, *Acanthodactylus scutellatus*, and the Desert Monitor, *Varanus griseus*. Twelve species of mammals have been recorded in the depressions but none is specific to this eco-zone. Henley's Dipodil, *Dipodillus henleyi*, is found here together with the Nile Rat, *Arvicanthus niloticus*, and the Swamp Cat, *Felis chaus*. While the Nile Rat may have been introduced, it is possible that the Swamp Cat in Farafra and Dakhla Oases is a relict species.

Of the smaller depressions, Wadi El Natrun is 50km long and a maximum of 8km wide. In early pharaonic times natron, a naturally occurring chemical mixture of carbonates, chlorides and sulphates, was mined here for use in the mummification process. Since the fourth century of our era the wadi has been noted for its association with the Christian Church.

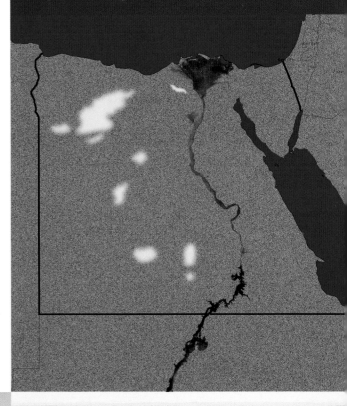

There are seven major depressions in the Western Desert, of which the most northerly and by far the largest is Qattara.

Rüppell's Sand Fox, *Vulpes rueppelli*: A small fox with large ears and an extremely bushy tail. The most ubiquitous of foxes in Egypt, it is found throughout the Western Desert and the oases. It appears to have little fear of humans and will come close to campsites to scavenge for food scraps and although mostly nocturnal, it is sometimes seen during the day.

Cream-colored Courser, *Cursorius cursor*: The sandy coloration of this slender, upright, long-legged, ground nester acts as perfect camouflage for the young. If the nest is approached, the young will remain absolutely still until almost stepped on before they run. The Courser's preferred habitat is open sandy desert or semi-desert with scant vegetation and its diet consists mainly of insects or occasionally other invertebrates.

Green Toad, *Bufo viridis*: A widespread amphibian of fresh and brackish water the Green Toad finds suitable habitat in the oases and depressions. There is a marked difference between the sexes; the males are smaller and of slenderer habit. They are varied in color and pattern. This toad of Palearctic affinity appears to be a relict species from a damper period in Egypt.

Mindy's Gecko, *Tarentola mindiae*: This newly discovered species of gecko was named only in 1997 and is distributed round the Qattara Depression. Despite being a desert dweller, it is largely confined to trees and shrubs found in the desert such as *Acacia* spp. and *Tamarix* spp. on which it is found in dense populations. The dark color and rough texture blend with the bark of the trees on which it lives.

Nile Tamarisk, *Tamarix nilotica*: This is a multiform plant that may grow as a shrub or a tree of 5–8m high. The tiny, scale-like leaves are gray-green in color and are sometimes covered in salt crystals. The pink flowers grow in long spikes and have a sweet scent. These trees are tolerant of saline soil and grow well where there is water.

Rose of Jericho, *Anastatica hierochuntica*: Mary is said to have clutched this plant while giving birth to Jesus. Thus its Arabic name is *Kaff Mariam* (the Hand of Mary). In the dry season, the leaf stems curl round the seeds to protect them. When it rains, the stems uncurl and release the seeds, which grow into small leafy green plants with white flowers.

Due to its relatively high rainfall, the coastal belt that extends **from Alexandria west** to Salum, is characterized by the richest and most diverse flora in Egypt except for that of Gebel Elba. The dunes of white sand by the sea are followed further inland by limestone ridges separated by wadis in some of which salt marshes are found. Inland of these is a relatively flat strip of *hamada* (sand and clay interspersed with exposed rocky surfaces). The people of this zone graze their livestock here and practice small-scale agriculture, growing dates, olives and figs among other crops. In addition there is considerable tourism development along this stretch of coast.

The vegetation of this zone includes nine plants that are endemic to Egypt. Of these four are found only along this stretch of coastline. Among them are an endemic variety, *Zygophyllum album* var. *album* and a full species of the same genus, *Z. aegyptium*. Also along this coastal desert is an endemic globe thistle, *Echinops taeckholmianus*, named for a famous botanist of Egypt, the late Dr. Vivi Täckholm.

The abundance of vegetation and temperate climate of this zone allow a rich assemblage of reptiles and mostly small mammals together with a high number of breeding birds. Many of these birds are restricted to this zone. During the autumn and spring migration seasons many millions of birds make landfall along the coast, which is their first resting place after crossing the Mediterranean or the great desert to the south. In one year the number of migrating Short-toed Larks, *Calandrella cinerea*, was estimated at 10,000 birds per square mile in a typical area west of Alexandria. The Cream-colored Courser, *Cursorius cursor*, is a characteristic resident of this area together with Dupont's Lark, *Chersophilus duponti*, Thekla Lark, *Galerida theklae*, and the Red-rumped Wheatear, *Oenanthe moesta*. The Raven, *Corvus corax*, is not known from elsewhere in Egypt.

Among the reptiles, the Moorish Gecko, *Tarentola mauritanica*, the Egyptian Leopard Lizard, *Acanthodactylus pardalis*, Changeable Agama, *Trapelus mutabilis*, and the Javelin Sand Boa, *Eryx jaculus*, a nocturnal, gecko-eating constrictor, are typical of this zone.

Among typical mammals of this zone are several endangered species of rodents including the Four-toed Jerboa, *Allactaga tetradactyla*, Greater Egyptian Jerboa, *Jaculus orientalis*. The fascinating Mole Rat, *Spalax ehrenbergi*, a blind, tailless, fossorial animal spends most of its life underground. The Mole Rat's vestigial eyes are covered with hairy skin and although it is totally unable to see, it is known to be active above ground when mating or occasionally to find edible vegetation. The Red Fox, *Vulpes vulpes*, and the Long-eared Hedgehog, *Hemiechinus auritus*, are also known from this area as well as the Fat Sand Rat, *Psammomys obesus*.

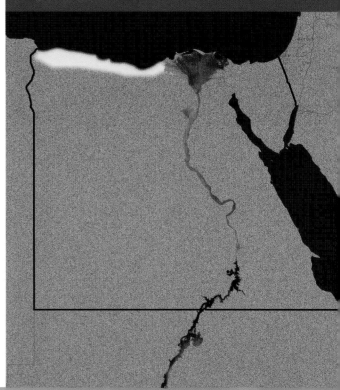

The coastal belt that extends from Alexandria west to Salum, is characterized by the richest and most diverse flora in Egypt except for that of Gebel Elba.

Desert Monitor, _Varanus griseus_: This large lizard is a common, diurnal denizen of desert and scrub terrain throughout Egypt. It is a predatory carnivore and appears to feed mainly on other lizards, snakes and rodents. The monitors are the only lizards that have long forked tongues like snakes and the animal is able to withdraw the tongue into a sheath at its base.

Long-eared Hedgehog, _Hemiechinus auritus_: This nocturnal animal is not a true desert hedgehog and is seen in more densely vegetated areas of the coastal desert. It sometimes digs a shallow burrow but is more often found in buildings, small caves or the burrows of other animals. The diet is largely insects and small vertebrates. Hedgehogs often suffer from infestation by ticks and fleas.

Quail, _Coturnix coturnix_: The smallest of the European game birds and the only one that migrates. Quails are ground nesters and can often be seen skulking in vegetation; if flushed they fly up with a loud whirring sound. Owing to their chubby build they depend on the wind to assist them in their migration and are often exhausted when they arrive in Egypt.

Desert Snail, _Eremina desertorum_: The most common terrestrial gastropod mollusks in the region, these snails are seen in millions on the ground in the area and the broken shells of dead individuals are so thoroughly mixed with the soil that it is sometimes referred to as 'snail soil.' Terrestrial gastropods have closeable lungs instead of the gills with which their marine relatives are provided.

Tamarisk, _Tamarix aphylla_: A widespread, stout tree in sandy habitats that can grow to 12m. The leaves are sheath-like without blades, which gives the tree the appearance of being leafless. This species is used as fuel, for medicinal purposes and for sand stabilization. Like other _Tamarix_ spp. it is able to tolerate saline conditions where the groundwater is within reach of its roots.

Ice Plant, _Mesembryanthemum crystallinum_: This stout succulent plant was originally introduced into Egypt as an ornamental but has now become completely naturalized. It is characterized by the glittering water-filled papillae that cover the foliage. The white flowers appear daisy-like but the numerous 'petals' are actually staminodes or modified stamens. The Ice plant forms large low-lying mats of ground cover.

Mediterranean Marine Habitats

The **Mediterranean coast** of Egypt runs 1200km, from Rafah on the border with the Gaza Strip to Salum at the Egyptian-Libyan border. Inshore the land slopes more or less steeply depending on where it is along the coastline. The 100m depth of the water is closer to the shore to the west and the distance gradually increases to the east. At Port Said it is furthest from the shore and further east it becomes closer again. This is caused by the alluvial cone that has built up in front of the mouth of the Nile in the Delta area.

The flora and fauna of the coastal waters are affected by the depth of the water and available food sources. In this zone, the biodiversity is relatively lower than in the Red Sea with primary food sources such as planktonic fauna and flora being limited. However, fairly extensive meadows of the sea grass, *Posidonia oceanica* and other species are found together with some brown algae such as *Sargassum* spp. especially along the western sector of the coast. Several species of red and green algae are also found. The sea grasses are vital as nurseries and sources of food for a variety of both invertebrates and vertebrates including the endangered Green Turtle, *Chelonia mydas*, the only one of the sea turtles that is almost exclusively vegetarian.

The benthic or bottom-feeding fauna is also greatly influenced by the type of bottom. Thus a sandy or silty bottom is suitable for certain species of echinoderms, mollusks and polychaetes, while a more stony bottom suits different species.

The invertebrate fauna of the southeastern Mediterranean is also relatively less diverse but includes a variety of mollusks (the largest group inshore), echinoderms and polychaetes (the largest group offshore). Other invertebrates including sponges, bryozoans, and crustaceans are also found in this zone. Four species of commercially important sponges: *Spongia officinalis*, *S. agarcinia*, *S. zimocca*, and *Hippospongia communis*, have been recorded from Egyptian waters of the Mediterranean.

There are no true stony corals in the Mediterranean; however, there are several species of bryozoans. These are tiny, sessile (immobile), colonial animals that are usually less than half a millimeter long. Most of the bryozoans form flat colonies that will encrust almost any hard surfaces such as shipwrecks, underwater cables and rocks. Other species form plant-like structures or erect plates and are called 'lace corals.'

Among the vertebrates, there are over 350 species of fish in Egyptian waters, of which about 43 are Indo-Pacific species that have migrated through the Suez Canal. Many of these fish are commercially important including various species of Rabbit Fish, Mullet, Sea Bass, and Groupers. Eight species of marine mammals have been recorded and, additionally, it is possible that the rare Monk Seal, *Monachus monachus*, may still be found, in suitable habitat west of Mersa Matruh as it is occasionally found off the coast of Libya not far from the Egyptian border.

Three species of sea turtles are known from the area: the Green Turtle, *Chelonia mydas*, the Loggerhead Turtle, *Caretta caretta*, and the Leatherback Turtle, *Dermochelys coriacea*. The Green and Loggerhead Turtles breed sporadically along the Egyptian coast. The Leatherback has not been known to nest in Egyptian waters and is, indeed, the rarest of the three species.

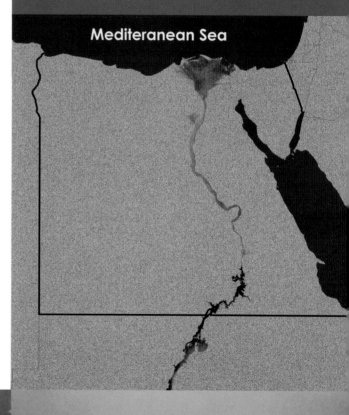

There are over 350 species of fish in the Egyptian Mediterranean; of these about 43 are Indo-Pacific species.

Mediteranean Sea

Grouper, *Epinephelus marginatus*: This is a commercially important group of fishes. They are carnivorous, feeding mainly on fishes and crustaceans. Groupers are protogynous hermaphrodites, meaning that they start maturity as females and later in life switch to become males. They are able to alter the density of the color very rapidly, for example when moving from a dark hole to a light-colored sandy area.

Greater Amberjack, *Seriola dumerilii*: These large, carnivorous pelagic fish are fast swimmers and voracious hunters that grow up to 2m in length. They are found in small groups around rocks in moderate to deep water. Juveniles differ from adults in coloration being yellow with dark vertical stripes. They sometimes hide under the bells of jellyfish or occasionally among shoals of Saure, *Boops salpa*.

Sea Grass, *Posidonia oceanica*: Almost 20% of all known Mediterranean species have been sighted in the sea grass meadows, which are thought to be the most important ecosystem in this sea. The mats of these plants play a major role in stabilizing sediment while the meadows temper water movement and help protect beaches. Sea grasses are the origin of a rich food web.

Slender-billed Gull, *Larus genei*: These gulls both winter and breed on the Mediterranean coast of Egypt in internationally important numbers. They are colonial nesters and often form large and noisy aggregations by fresh or brackish lakes or by coastal lagoons. Opportunist feeders, they will eat fish, crustaceans, mollusks, vegetable matter or even carrion. Both parents care for the 1 – 4 young.

Loggerhead Turtle, *Caretta caretta*: The Loggerheads are more dispersive than other sea turtles when away from the nesting beaches and their movements are not well known. The females lay four to five clutches of 72 – 130 eggs per season at 2 – 3 year intervals. Mainly carnivorous, they feed on benthic invertebrates like shrimps, squid, sea urchins, and sponges and occasionally seaweeds and sea grasses.

Coralligenous community: After the *Posidonia* meadows, this community constitutes the most important hot spot for species diversity in the Mediterranean. Lying between 20 and 130m it forms rims, rolls or tables along vertical walls. It harbors such invertebrates as large sponges, gorgonians and bryozoa and forms a spectacularly colored ecosystem. This ecosystem constitutes the main diving sites and is therefore of great economic importance.

Rüppell's Sand Fox, *Vulpes rueppelli*: The most ubiquitous fox in Egypt, it is found throughout the Eastern and Western Deserts and Sinai. It appears to have little fear of humans and will come close to campsites to scavenge for food scraps; although mostly nocturnal, it is sometimes seen during the day. It is hunted as a pest and for 'sport.'

Fennec Fox, *Vulpes zerda*: The huge ears of this nocturnal carnivore may assist heat dissipation and the palms and soles are covered by long hair, enabling it to run on soft sand. Despite their hardiness they are diminishing in numbers due to hunting and collection as pets and to a reduction in availability of the insect and small rodent food on which they live.

Nubian Ibex, *Capra nubiana*: These beautiful female ibex have smaller horns than the males and are safe on the mountain peaks where they live but are vulnerable when they come down to waterholes to drink. They have been hunted since prehistoric times but with modern weapons, the toll on their populations is becoming too great to sustain.

Lappet-faced Vulture, *Torgos tracheliotus*: The adult of this huge bird of prey has a wingspan of up to three meters and like similar large birds it has declined in numbers over the centuries and has disappeared from many parts of Egypt due to loss of habitat and to hunting because of its perceived predatory habits.

White-eyed Gull, *Larus leucophthalmus*: This gull is endemic to the Red Sea where about 30% of the world population nests on the islands at the mouth of the Gulf of Suez. These islands are fragile environments and are easily disrupted by human interference; even minimal negative interventions would seriously impact entire nesting colonies.

Green Turtle, *Chelonia mydas*: This juvenile, non-breeding Green Turtle is one of two species that nest along the Red Sea coast and is the only herbivorous marine turtle. These gentle animals are endangered because for centuries, they have been taken by fishermen for food and for their shells, which are valued for the fashion trade.

Barbary sheep, *Ammotragus lervia*: Aside from a very small population in the almost inaccessible Gilf Kebir, these hardy drought-tolerant animals were thought to have been hunted to extinction in Egypt. Recently, however, small populations have been found in mountainous terrain of the Eastern Desert, where they were formerly numerous. They are still seriously endangered

Dorcas Gazelle, *Gazella dorcas*: Despite their delicate and graceful appearance these animals are able to survive in very harsh and arid desert terrain. They are constantly at risk from illegal hunting. Egyptian Bedouins largely practice sustainable hunting for food but no such considerations restrain large, well-equipped hunting parties from abroad.

Egyptian Tortoise, *Testudo kleinmanni*: This small, vegetarian tortoise is extremely endangered due to its popularity with the pet trade. It is mainly endemic to Libya and Egypt; in Egypt its range is restricted to the Mediterranean coastal deserts. A small population is still extant in North Sinai and is currently the subject of conservation efforts.

Dugong, *Dugong dugon*: The Dugong is a completely aquatic herbivore; its only food is the seagrass, *Halodule uninervis*. It is therefore dependant on the seagrass beds for sustenance. Much of the world's oil passes along the Red Sea; even a minor oil spill could adversely affect this endangered mammal, which is also hunted for food.

Argun Palm, *Medemia argun*: Probably the rarest plant in Egypt, the whole population of this palm is confined to a few individuals in Dunqul Oasis. A careless camper could wipe out the entire population. Its numbers are diminishing throughout its range and, as propagation is slow, it is listed by the IUCN as endangered.

Ombet Tree, *Dracaena ombet*: This small tree with rosettes of sword-shaped leaves and pink flowers is, in Egypt, found only at higher elevations on Gebel Elba. It was believed to be an endemic species but is found in the southwestern Arabian Peninsula, Sudan and Ethiopia. It has been listed by the IUCN as an endangered species.

Egypt is unique in that it forms a land bridge between Africa and Eurasia and has been crossed and re-crossed by migratory peoples since the dawn of time. Some of those people found the land good and stayed. About 5000 B.C. or earlier, agriculture was introduced in the Nile Valley and has continued to the present time changing its character into what is now essentially a man-made environment. The people who did this still live in the Nile Valley and still till its rich soil.

The Western Desert was crossed by the caravan routes of people from the Western Sahara, some of whom stayed for longer or shorter periods of time depending on the benefits such as good grazing or opportunities for raiding the rich caravans from the Nile Valley. Some of the people who live today in the oases of the Western Desert are descended from these pastoral nomads and raiders. However, it is only in Siwa Oasis that there are Berbers who still speak the Berber language. People from the Nile Valley have also settled in the oases. Along the Mediterranean Coastal Desert, the land was settled by Arabs who came from the Arabian Peninsula in the wake of the conquest of Egypt by Amr Ibn El Aas in the seventh century.

In the southern part of the Eastern Desert live a Hamitic people whose origins are lost in the mists of time. These people are the Bisharin who speak a unique language called Beja. The Bisharin share their territory with a group of people of Arab origin called the Rashida, who travel from the Sudan with their camels. Further north the tribes are Bedouin Arabs who have migrated over the centuries from the Arabian Peninsula. To the northeast on the Sinai Peninsula, the people are also Arabs.

All of these diverse groups interact in one way or another with the land on which they live. In the Nile Valley, the people substantially changed the environment from a rich natural river oasis to an equally rich cultivated river oasis. In other parts of Egypt, such a change has not been possible so the people who live on the land have found it necessary to conserve the resources they have in order to maximize the benefits they gain from those resources.

Conservation, therefore, was traditionally a matter of maintaining the fauna and flora in order to maintain their way of life. It is not so much what they do, but what they do not do. Instead of cutting down living trees to obtain fodder, the branches are shaken so that the leaves, on which the goats and sheep feed, fall to the ground. Cutting trees for charcoal is also frowned upon. Hunting wild animals is generally limited to the number of animals needed for food. Harvesting plants for food, fuel or medicine is also more or less regulated. The pastoral nomad knows only too well that if his flocks overgraze an area, there will be fewer plants the next time there is rain.

With the advent of modern technology and more government intervention, such as the introduction of health clinics and schools in villages and towns, land use patterns are changing and many of the formerly nomadic and semi-nomadic people of Egypt are now living in settlements. The old ways of conserving the often-fragile ecosystems are no longer sufficient. The Government of Egypt is introducing some innovative programs through which the people will maintain an interest in their environment and culture and in the importance of maintaining and preserving them.

Diverse groups of people interact with the land in order to protect it.

Medicinal Plants

In the ninth year of the reign of *Amenophis* I (c. 1550 B.C.), about 900 remedies were being used by physicians.

From earliest times the **Ancient Egyptians** were renowned for their knowledge of medicinal plants. By the time the Papyrus Ebers was compiled in the ninth year of the reign of *Amenophis* I (c. 1550 B.C.), about 900 remedies were being used by physicians. The majority of these remedies were derived from plants and about 150 of the plants are said to have been identified with reasonable accuracy. Some 700 years after this marvelous work was achieved, the Greek poet, Homer, wrote in the *Odyssey* of "the many useful drugs, which had been given to the daughter of Zeus [Helen] by an Egyptian lady, Polydamna, the wife of *Thoth*."

The Bedouins and other indigenous people of Egypt continue to practice herbal medicine and to use plants that they know are effective remedies for various ailments. There are also traditional healers called *Hukamaa* (singular: *Hakim*) who administer traditional remedies for minor ailments although for more serious illnesses the Bedouin increasingly tend to go to government clinics when they are within reach.

The Government of Egypt is currently undertaking a project to conserve globally significant medicinal plant species. The project aims to stop the use of critically endangered plant species in hotspots; introduce community-based, small-scale cultivation, processing, and marketing of medicinal plants to relieve pressure on wild sources, and introduce best practice for sustainable collection of wild medicinal plants in the protected areas. It will also promote alternative energy sources in demonstration areas, disperse grazing pressure, protect community intellectual property rights, and replicate project successes throughout Egypt.

Forty-two species have been targeted for special attention during the course of the project. Of these, all are vulnerable, endangered or rare and 16 species are endemic. Several species are either exported or sold in local markets in relatively large quantities.

There is a number of threats to medicinal plants that have not so far been addressed but will be under this project. Among these are: over collection, trade in medicinal plants, fuel collection, and overgrazing.

There is a small but expanding private sector trade in the cultivation and processing of medicinal plants. Cosmetic products such as soaps are now available in the market as well as many culinary herbs. The Egypt Bio-Dynamic Association (EBDA) has established Sekem, a private-sector corporation, which in partnership with farmers has established more than 150 farms of medicinal plants in various parts of Egypt.

Many of the plants that are listed in the Papyrus Ebers are still in use today. They are used for a variety of purposes including slimming and treating ailments such as skin diseases, intestinal parasites, rheumatism, urinary tract diseases and many others. Plants are also used to make such diverse products as leather dye, soap and hair tonic. The Conservation and Sustainable Use of Medicinal Plants project will benefit many people and is an important enterprise not least because the loss of this valuable natural resource would be a tragedy for all concerned.

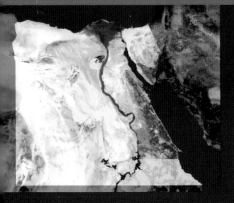

The Bishari, who occupy the land from Baranis south to Port Sudan area, are descended from Neolithic tribal groups of ancient Hamitic origin and may have belonged in the area for more than 4000 years. They have a close affinity with their environment and the responsibility they feel for it is rooted in their ancient heritage.

Painting: A characteristic Bishari summer camp to which the family returns from time to time. The *Balanites aegyptiaca* tree is used to support the simple shelter designed to provide shade while allowing maximum cooling airflow.

Photographs: A shelter in the desert is used by shepherds for shade (1). In the camp, intricately woven Acacia branches form the roofs of dwellings and belongings are placed on top to help provide insulation against the heat of the day (2). This is appreciated by two Bishari tribesmen who enjoy some coolness under the shady roof, which is supported by wishbone poles (3). Outside the camp small, carefully demarcated areas of clean sand are used as *Mussalaya*, the Bishari equivalent of prayer mats (4). A Bishari compound has a winter room on the left and a summer room on the right (5), while in another compound the winter dwelling is covered with cloth, animal skins and a fabric of woven palm fronds. The cloth and the palm frond fabric are imported from elsewhere in Egypt (6).The Bishari people have distinctive features and often wear

these beautifully ornamented combs in their hair (7). They also like to decorate their camel saddles with their intricate and colorful leather craftsmanship (8), their winter dwellings are covered with fabrics and animal skins. Camel or goat hair fabric is also used for bright geometrically patterned rugs (9).

Tribesmen enjoy a traditional dance with a sword and a weapon that is a type of quarterstaff (10). Sheikh Hassan, the leader of the Gebel Elba Bishari with young men who are holding ancient weaponry such as the sword with the leaf-shaped blade and a unique shield made from an elephant's ear (11). Dancing and music are integral to life in the desert and among these artifacts is a type of lyre called a *Rababa* (12).

While the men hunt and take care of trading, the women, like this elderly lady, look after the goats and long-tailed Sudanese sheep (13). This little boy is resting his arms on the staff that no Bishari man is ever without; it is used as a walking stick or to lean on as well as to rest the arms on. At need, it can be a weapon. The Saluki-like dogs are used as guard dogs and sheepdogs as well as for hunting (14).

The Ababda are of African descent. They have developed a way of life that suits them and the barren landscape in which they live. The Ababda have a strong conservation ethic with individual families taking responsibility for conserving the resources of specified areas.

Painting: An Ababda compound showing a unique traditional tent of camel hair with a windbreak at one side. Arak, *Salvadora persica*, bushes are behind the tent; in the foreground there is a traditional loom and a tiny tent for young goats. To the right, an open-sided shade similar to that of the Bashari has belongings piled on top for insulation and safety; a fishing net hangs at one side.

Photographs: Nothing is wasted in the desert; the windbreak shown here is made of non-traditional plastic sheet (1) and the shelter with wishbone supporting connectors is similar to that of the Bishari (2). To all desert-dwellers the spiritual life is very important. Ababdas are devout Muslims, this man prays in a *mussalaya* integrated with a grave (3). The placing of grave goods dates back to Pharaonic times. These items belonged to the deceased person; they are placed in the grave or tomb and include comestibles such as salt, sugar and coffee as well as money (4).
Ababda compound with a woodpile for firewood and for building.(5) A sheikh's tomb

with demarcated area and white flags to identify it as a tomb (6). A young woman with the characteristic African features of the Ababda (7). The nose ring and hair ornament worn by this elderly woman are also characteristic of the Ababda (8). Social life within the tribe is of great importance, as can be seen from this family group, gathered to drink the local coffee, known as *Gabbana*. Coffee drinking is almost a ritual with its own unique utensils (9). Another vital feature of desert life is the water well where the people draw water and exchange news (10).

A handshake seals the sale of charcoal (11), the making of which impacts the environment and negatively influences the cultural landscape (12). That this spring has been used for many centuries is shown by the façade that was carved round it in Ptolemaic times. It is the source of the pool by which an Ababda tribesman exchanges news with a Bishari (13). The Ababda are proud of their area's long history. This man in a traditional vest called *sidiery* and a long robe *(galabeya)* points out the prehistoric rock art (14).

For millennia, groups of Arabs have migrated into Egypt from the Arabian Peninsula. They came to escape tribal wars or to trade and later in the wake of the seventh century Arab conquest of Egypt. They are now part of the cultural fabric of this land. In the Eastern Desert the Ma'aza tribe is important while the Rashida, based around Kassala in Sudan, bring their camels and goods to market in Shalateen. The Bedouin tribes of the Sinai are the bridge between Arabia and Egypt and the Awlad Ali has settled mainly along the Mediterranean coast.

Painting: Rashida compound with a windbreak in the foreground and a woman in characteristic dress selling fabric. In the center two men perform a sword dance; one is kicking up sand while he slashes vigorously with his sword. The tent on the left is traditional camel hair while that on the right is a contemporary version. Behind the tents are Oshar, *Calotropis procera*, trees.

Photographs: Traditional hair tents are part of a row, shown in photograph number 6, that have been arranged for a wedding celebration in South Sinai (1). Among the foods eaten in North Sinai will be these melon seeds being dried in the hot, clean desert sand (2). That everything could be utilized can be seen from this dwelling made of various local plants in North Sinai (3) and from the plastic sheeting that is used to line the permeable sand for water storage; a system known as *Maknaz el Maya* (4).

Shrines are constructed in a burial area of Nabi Salah in St Katherine Protectorate (5). A row of less permanent tents is arranged for a traditional wedding celebration of the Elaygat tribe (6). Daily chores still need to be done and this little girl feeds a goat with soaked date pits in North Sinai (7). A Rashida woman wears traditional dress and has tribal markings on her face (8) but the traveling department store that serves Bedouin communities is nowadays in the back of a pick-up truck (9). More traditionally, Rashida tribesmen bring their camel caravan from Sudan to market in Egypt (10). This Bedouin woman's traditional dress and accessories includes fifteen different items (11). The beautifully decorated dresses of the dancing women are shown off at a Bedouin wedding in South Sinai (12) and the making of coffee for which these utensils are required (13) is the hallmark of Bedouin hospitality in North Sinai.

The settled people of the Nile Valley and Delta have cultivated the fertile soil for millennia.

Photographs: The characteristic features of Nile Valley dwellers (1) can be seen on these farmers transporting freshly cut alfalfa (*Barseem*) (2). A characteristic of the North Delta people is a love of color (3). Another dress, being shown off at a farmer's market in the North Delta is unique (4). A love for beauty is evident in the lines of this Felucca on which the rudder forms a decorative element (5) and even the humble and somewhat faded donkey cart (*Carro*) is still colorful (6).

The Berbers are an ancient people of North African origin. They live in the Siwa Oasis region and still speak the Berber language.

Photographs: Sheikh Hassan of the tiny Qara Oasis is a much respected leader (1). Children waving cheerfully from their *Carro* in Siwa (2).This colorful woven camel-hair fabric is used for many purposes, not least nowadays, to make attractive souvenirs for tourists (3). One of many such hot springs in Siwa, this one is used for bathing and irrigation (4). The tomb of a virtuous Sheikh is decorated with ostrich eggs. (5). A shop in Siwa sells local crafts like that in photograph number 3 (6).

Nature Conservation Sector

Objectives

Egypt is rich in natural resources, especially marine corals and desert ecosystems both of which are delicate and need special care. Conservation of these resources is being challenged by rapid population growth and the massive size of the development needed to support it. The Nature Conservation Sector was set up with the objective of protecting, promoting and maintaining the natural heritage of Egypt. Under the aegis of the NCS, conservation efforts are being carried out within the framework of management of the Protected Areas and the various conservation projects that are currently underway and through the enforcement of laws and regulations. The immediate objectives of the NCS are as follows:

- Establishment of a representative Protected Area Network;
- Managing these areas to conserve biological diversity and protect natural values;
- Ensuring that income generation for the use of Protected Areas is maximized without prejudice to the maintenance of natural values and that this income is used to manage the areas;
- Promoting the conservation and sustainable use of natural resources outside protected areas in cooperation with other stakeholders.

Strategy and Action plan

A National Strategy and Action Plan for Biodiversity Conservation was prepared to meet Egypt's commitments under the Convention on Biological Diversity (CBD). The plan covers the period from 1997 to 2017 and sets goals for the protection of ecosystems and their sustainable management.

From Rio to Johannesburg: Achievements in Implementation of the CBD

In 1992, the United Nations Conference on Environment and Development (UNCED) in Rio de Janeiro was hailed as giving hope for the world's rapidly deteriorating environment. At that conference Agenda 21, the action plan for a sustainable future, was endorsed. Ten years on, the World Summit on Sustainable Development has taken place in Johannesburg from August 26 to September 4, 2002. This summit was an opportunity to reinvigorate political commitment to the goals set forth at Rio and to move from concepts to action.

Egypt was represented both at Rio and at Johannesburg and during the intervening ten years has made steady progress towards implementing the programs necessary to fulfill the commitments made at Rio. The Protected Area Network has developed dramatically. Many projects for the sustainable development of Egypt's rich wildlife resources are either already underway or are at the planning stage.

The Nature Conservation Sector was set up with the objective of protecting, promoting and maintaining the natural heritage of Egypt.

Protected Areas

To date, the nature conservation efforts in Egypt have focused mainly on the establishment of a Protected Areas Network, representative of the nation's ecosystems, which aims to maintain the diversity and viability of Egypt's natural heritage and its sustainable utilization. During the past two decades, since the passage of law 102/1983 concerning the establishment of Protected Areas, twenty-four Protected Areas have been declared, covering an area of 91,000km^2 or 9% of the land area of Egypt. These are some of the most beautiful and precious parts of the country. The Protected Area Network as it stands today has a good representation of the various habitats and ecosystems of Egypt, however, there are some further important hotspots, which will be included in the future. Plans are in place to increase the number of Protectorates to 40 and the land area covered to 17% by the year 2017.

Most recently Siwa Oasis, the White Desert and Wadi Gemal/Hamata were added to Egypt's Protected Areas Network. A high priority is the establishment of a marine protected area along the Egyptian coast of the Red Sea. This would provide an effective management tool to maintain the coral reef systems of the Red Sea, which constitute Egypt's most valuable biodiversity resource.

Biodiversity is not the only natural resource protected areas aim to conserve; outstanding landscapes and geological formations are also taken into consideration. There are four protected areas that were designated primarily for their geological significance and unique landscapes, most notably the White Desert. Cultural heritage, which abounds in every part of Egypt, also receives high consideration. Local people and their cultures, together with potential utility for eco-tourism are also important aspects of the protected areas.

Much effort has been invested in the management of protected areas, so that they fulfill their objectives. Today many of the sites have effective management plans, infrastructure, and equipment and are run by professional staff. These protected areas have become an integral part of the nation's landscape and have started to show results. In 2001, 1.25 million people visited Egypt's protected areas.

Egypt's protected areas not only aim to preserve biodiversity and other aspects of natural heritage but also aim to maximize benefits to society and local communities by harnessing, in innovative and ecologically sensitive ways, the natural conditions they maintain. Protected areas have also proved to be an effective regional land-use planning tool, for example in South Sinai, where a unique partnership between tourism and conservation has evolved, each benefiting from the other. The philosophy of the NCS is that the protected area status granted to some regions of the country is a genuine type of land use that is economically viable and sustainable in the long term, and should not be viewed as a means of hindering development.

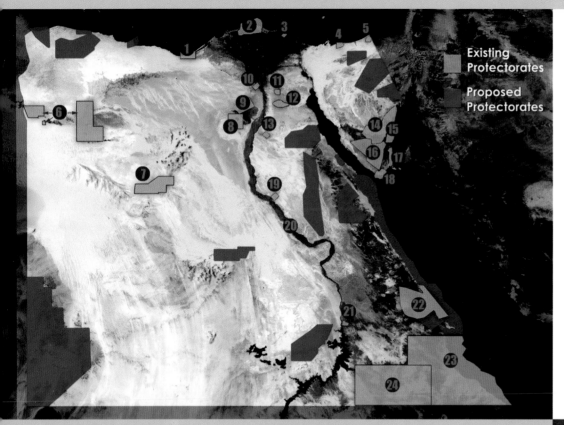

Existing Protectorates

Proposed Protectorates

Laws and Regulations

The Government of Egypt has passed a number of laws concerned with nature conservation and environmental affairs.

Law 53/1966. The Agricultural Law

While Law 53/1966 was not the first Egyptian law with provisions for the protection of wildlife, however it superseded previous laws that had addressed the matter. This law has a number of provisions for the protection of endangered reptiles, mammals and birds and refers particularly to the protection of birds that are beneficial to agriculture.

Law 102/1983. For Protected Areas

Law 102/1983 is the cornerstone of modern conservation efforts in Egypt. It established the legal framework that enabled the Government of Egypt to create and manage protected areas in the country. The law specified the criteria by which such areas should be chosen. They are to be areas of land or water that have value for fauna, flora or geological interest. They could also be of value for culture, science, aesthetics and tourism. Within these areas human activity should be strictly regulated and hunting prohibited. The Law designated the EEAA as the government body responsible for the selection and management of protected areas.

Law 124/1983 on Catching Fish and Aquatic Life

This law regulates harvesting of fish and other aquatic organisms in marine and inland waters, as well as aquaculture. It specifies standards for fishing methods, bans certain illegal techniques and fishing gear, and establishes a licensing system for fishing and aquaculture. The provisions of this law are implemented by the General Authority for the Development of Fisheries Resources of the Ministry of Agriculture.

Law 4/1994. For the Environment

Law 4/1994 is the most significant piece of legislation concerning the environment in Egypt. The EEAA was designated as the government body concerned with the implementation of the law.

Although Law 4/1994 is largely concerned with issues of pollution, it also addresses hunting of wildlife forbidding the hunting of specified animals

The El Omayed Biosphere Reserve covers 700 km² of the Mediterranean Coastal Desert, and contains some of the most abundant and diverse flora in Egypt. The reserve consists of two core areas; transition zones, where some activities are permitted and a buffer zone that allows for small-scale traditional agriculture.

Three main topographical zones are the coastal dunes, limestone ridges and depressions and the inland plateau. These habitats hold endemic plants. The endangered Four-toed Jerboa, *Allactaga tetradactyla*, is found here.

Lake Burullus is east of the Rosetta branch of the Nile. It is shallow and rather elongated; about 50 small islands are scattered through it; there is one connection with the sea. Salinity is high to the northeast and decreases to the south. Commercial salt production and fish farming are carried on to the south. The southern shore is bordered by reed swamps and abundant aquatic vegetation grows underwater.

The lake is an important wetland for wintering waterfowl including Wigeon, *Anas penelope*, and Ferruginous Duck, *Aythya nyroca*.

Ashtum El Gamil is a small protected area at the eastern end of the sandbar that separates Lake Manzala from the Mediterranean and was declared mainly to protect gravid fish and fry as they pass in and out of the lake. The possible enlargement of this protected area will greatly increase its importance.

Lake Manzala is Egypt's most important wetland for wintering waterbirds and holds up to a quarter of a million birds annually, including vast concentrations of Little Gull, *Larus minuta*, and Whiskered Tern, *Chlidonias hybridus*.

The White Desert, one of the most recently protected areas, lies completely within the depression of Farafra, running north of Qasr Farafra to the northeastern escarpment. The white chalk of the depression is dotted with inselbergs embedded with numerous fossil seashells; the ground is scattered with thousands of oxidized iron pyrites concretions. The protected area includes two small, uninhabited oases, Wadi Hennis and Karawein Depression. Very large, old specimens of *Acacia nilotica here* are of special scientific interest.

Wadi El Rayan is a small depression southwest of El Fayoum. Two man-made lakes, created by agricultural run-off water from El Fayoum, are joined by a channel and a small waterfall. The upper lake is densely vegetated with *Phragmites* and *Tamarix*. The lower lake is brackish and its shores are poorly vegetated. Zeuglodon Valley, nearby, is famous for the fossil whales found there, especially *Basilosaurus isis*.

The lakes are wintering habitat for waterbirds, including Ferruginous Duck, *Aythya nyroca*. The Slender-horned Gazelle, *Gazella leptoceros*, is probably locally extinct.

Lake Qarun has been a source of fish and a habitat for waterfowl since time immemorial. The lake's main water source is drainage from agricultural land, which enters through two major drains called El Batts and El Wadi. This water has become increasingly saline as agriculture has intensified and the water is now more saline than seawater. Freshwater fish and invertebrates have largely disappeared and marine species have been introduced. This lake is of international importance for wintering waterbirds including Black-necked Grebe, *Podiceps nigricollis*, and Northern Shoveller, *Anas clypeata*.

Zaranik lies at the eastern end of Lake Bardawil and is a major bottleneck for migrating waterbirds due to its location and the Zaranik Lagoon. Small islets in the lagoon support dense halophytic vegetation.

Recently, a very small population of the rare and endangered Egyptian Tortoise, *Testudo kleinmanni*, has been found in the area and Loggerhead Turtle, *Caretta caretta*, has been found to nest on the Mediterranean shore. Several vulnerable or threatened species of birds migrate through the area including Corncrake, *Crex crex*, and Pallid Harrier, *Circus macrourus*.

El Ahrash is an area of Mediterranean coastal sand dunes of up to 60m high that have moderately good cover of herbs, grasses and trees including *Acacia* and *Tamarix* spp. Some of the vegetation in the area has been cultivated for sand stabilization and to provide fodder for livestock.

The vegetation provides food and cover for wild animals and birds but it also provides firewood as well as grazing for local communities. Overgrazing and over collection of firewood, as a result, is threatening this already fragile coastal ecosystem.

Siwa Oasis, located between the Libyan border and the Qattara Depression in northwest Egypt, is important for its faunal and cultural diversity. Siwa has many lakes and over a thousand springs but the water is very saline and supports little agriculture except dates, olives and a few vegetables.

Siwa supports the endangered Slender-horned Gazelle, *Gazella leptoceros*, and Fennec Fox, *Vulpes zerda*. It may still be home to the Cheetah, *Acinonyx jubatus*, one of the most threatened cats in the world. Typical birds include the Turtle Dove, *Streptopelia turtur*.

El Hassana Dome was created by contortions of the earth's crust that caused Cretaceous limestone, 135 million years old, to break through younger formations. At El Hassana, north of Cairo a dome-like structure stands alone in the predominantly Eocene plateau of about 50 million years old. The contortions and folding are quite clearly visible in the dome in which numerous marine fossils are embedded.

Despite the aridity of the area, there is some vegetation, as well as lizards and the ubiquitous White-crowned Black Wheatear, *Oenanthe leucopyga*.

Maadi Petrified Forest is the remnants of a forest that grew 35 million years ago during a wetter period in Egypt. Great geological upheavals were taking place as the Red Sea was formed by the separation of the African and Arabian tectonic plates.

The wadi is moderately vegetated and among the wildlife is Cape Hare, *Lepus capensis*, and small rodents like the Cairo Spiny Mouse, *Acomys cahirinus*. Birds are generally those of the Eastern Desert including Mourning Wheatear, *Oenanthe lugens*. Among reptiles there is the Pale Agama, *Trapelus pallidus*.

Wadi Degla rises in the mountains of the Eastern Desert and runs northwest to the Nile Valley just south of Cairo at Maadi. It runs through limestone terrain cutting a deep winding canyon; in parts, floodwaters have carved the rock into spectacular shapes. There are numerous fossils in the rock formations and scattered patches of petrified wood.

After rain, ephemeral plants carpet the wadi. Dorcas Gazelle, *Gazella dorcas*, and Nubian Ibex, *Capra nubiana*, have been reported in recent years; bats live in the caves in the wadi sides.

Sannur Cave is a classic karst cave created by groundwater percolating through the Eocene limestone of the Galala Plateau. It is the only example of this phenomenon in Egypt. As the water percolates downwards, excess calcium carbonates are deposited on the roof and floor of the cave forming spectacular stalactites and stalagmites of various forms. When a light is shone on them, they glitter like a wonderland. Above ground, there are deposits of the red soil (terra rossa) associated with such formations as well as several swallow-holes (dolines).

Taba Protected Area is the northernmost protected area in South Sinai with desert landscapes, steep-walled wadis and high mountains. It is one of the most untouched areas in South Sinai and includes critical environments such as freshwater springs. Nawamis, the oldest stone-roofed buildings in the world, are found here.

Sinai Leopard, *Panthera pardus jarvisi*, may still be extant in the protectorate. Black Eagle, *Aquila verreauxii*, breeds here and possibly the rare Lammergeyer, *Gypaetus barbatus*. Twenty-four species of reptiles and up to 480 species of plants are found.

Abu Galum is the third of the five protected areas of South Sinai and is located to the north of Nabq. High coastal mountains are represented as well as the coral reefs for which the Red Sea is famous.

Along the Gulf of Aqaba the coastal plain is narrow and this protected area plays an important role in regulating land use. The Nubian Ibex, *Capra nubiana*, is found on virtually inaccessible peaks and the reefs are among the finest in the world and are still in pristine condition.

Wadi El Asyuti runs through the great limestone plateau of the Eastern Desert and debouches into the Nile Valley. This wadi is still largely undisturbed and supports a moderate amount of vegetation. The presence of water in small quantities is conducive to the survival of wildlife in the area including the Nubian Ibex, *Capra nubiana*, and the Caracal, *Caracal caracal*. Among reptiles are Jan's Cliff Racer, *Coluber rhodorhachis*, and Gray's Agama, *Agama spinosa*. Many small passerine species pass through the area during the biannual migration seasons.

50

The Nile River Islands Protected Area comprises about 144 islands dotted along the river and forming attractive habitat for wading birds and wintering habitat for waterfowl, due to the reed swamp of *Phragmites* and *Typha* that surrounds many of them. On some of the larger islands there are habitations and small-scale agriculture is practiced.

There are seasonal changes in the water level of the Nile and the resulting mudflats and sandy or muddy banks form habitat not only for wading birds but also for amphibians and freshwater invertebrates.

Saluga and Ghazal are two small granite islands in the Nile at Aswan. They support luxuriant natural vegetation; the last remnant of nilotic vegetation that dominated the Nile Valley before its complete modification by man. About 94 species are included in the flora and this has earned the islands their protected status.

Due to the abundance of characteristic nilotic flora the islands attract many bird species including wading birds. The protected status of the islands in this beautiful area is important to the maintenance of the natural landscape.

St Katherine Protectorate covers 4300km² of the mountains of South Sinai, encompassing the highest mountain in Egypt, Gebel Katherina, and Gebel Musa. The cultural history of the Protectorate is important to Islam, Christianity and Judaism and St Katherine's Monastery is the oldest continuously occupied monastery in the world.

The Protectorate contains over a quarter of the plants endemic to Egypt. Among the fauna are the rare Blanford's Fox, *Vulpes cana*, and an endemic species of butterfly, the Sinai Baton Blue, *Pseudophilotes sinaicus*, the smallest butterfly in the world.

Nabq lies at the narrowest part of the Gulf of Aqaba. This, the second of the five protected areas of South Sinai, holds one of the most northerly stands of Mangrove, *Avicennia marina*, in the world. Inland, the desert is well vegetated with Toothbrush Bush (Arak), *Salvadora persica*, and supports small numbers of Dorcas Gazelle, *Gazella dorcas*.

Marine creatures live and breed among the mangrove root systems while the crowns form nesting and feeding habitat for shore birds including Spoonbill, *Platalea leucorodia*, and Osprey, *Pandion haliaetus*.

Ras Mohamed is the fossil coral headland at the southernmost tip of Sinai and is poised between the rich coral reefs and the desert inland. At the southern end of the headland there is a small stand of Mangrove, *Avicennia marina*.

Beneath the crystal-clear water of the Red Sea are coral reefs teeming with life including a diversity of vertebrate and invertebrate species. Slightly further offshore dolphins, including Risso's Dolphin, *Grampus griseus*, are seen. The area hosts huge numbers of White Stork, *Ciconia ciconia*, during the annual migrations.

Wadi El Gemal/Hamata Protected Area covers some 4600km² of the Red Sea coast and includes the Wadi Gemal Island, coral reefs, seagrass beds and mangroves, together with Gebel Hamata (1977m), where ibex and gazelles are still found. Seagrasses feed the Dugong, *Dugong dugon*, and the Green Turtle, *Chelonia mydas*, which nests on the coast and island.

At the mouth of the wadi, a freshwater stream mingled with seawater forms a low-salinity marsh supporting reeds and Dôm Palms. Further inland are *Tamarix* spp., then *Balanites aegyptiaca* and the Toothbrush Bush, *Salvadora persica*.

The Elba Protected Area is unique in Egypt for its location between the Afrotropical and Saharo-Sindian regions. Gebel Elba, the centerpiece of the area, enjoys precipitation of up to 400mm annually, mostly mist, which creates mist oases.

The flora is the richest in Egypt but only one endemic, *Biscutella elbensis*, is found, also the rare Ombet Tree, *Dracaena ombet*. Mammals include two sub-Saharan species, Zoril, *Ictonyx striatus*, and Aardwolf, *Proteles cristatus*. Barbary Sheep, *Ammotragus lervia*, has recently been rediscovered. Many birds breed, in Egypt, only here.

Wadi El Allaqi covers a huge area between the western Red Sea mountains and the Nile Valley with habitats as diverse as its topography. Downstream, the wadi has been inundated by water from Lake Nasser and is known as Khor El Allaqi. In this area *Tamarix nilotica*, which can tolerate submergence when the water is high, dominates the flora.

The Khor is an important wetland for wintering wildfowl. Also found here are the Nile Monitor, *Varanus niloticus*, Nile Crocodile, *Crocodylus niloticus*, and the Nile Soft-shelled Turtle, *Trionyx triunguis*.

INVOLVING LOCAL COMMUNITIES

ACACIA REHABILITATION PROGRAM

SOUTH SINAI HANDICRAFTS PROJECT

Promoting the welfare of local people leads to the conservation of nature

The EEAA recognizes that the support and welfare of local communities are vital for the sustainable development of Egypt's protected areas along with the preservation of cultural traditions.

An example is the EEAA supported project for revitalizing traditional Bedouin crafts in south Sinai, a local income generating activity.

Without the involvement of local communities the conservation effort are likely to be doomed to failure. For this reason the NCS has given priority to the participation of local communities in conservation efforts. The following programs seek to involve local people: Construction, ownership and management of eco-lodges and other infrastructure; provision of trained Rangers and Community Guards for Protected Areas; provision of Guides for activity-based tourism; the 'Crafts for Conservation' program; stone carving using the beautiful local varieties of stone; the Acacia Rehabilitation Program and the Egyptian Tortoise Project

Owing to the loss of Acacia trees due to excessive cutting for fuel and for charcoal, a project has been initiated in South Sinai for the regeneration of Acacia populations. In coordination with the Suez Canal and Cairo universities, NCS staff members have conducted research on the rehabilitation of these trees and have planted over 35,000 seedlings since 2000.

The program involves local people who grow the seedlings in nurseries and are then responsible for managing the Acacia plantations. The people themselves are largely responsible for the continuing success of this program.

Crafts for Conservation is particularly aimed at women and assists them in preserving, developing and marketing their traditional skills, including their own special style of embroidered and beaded items, the motifs of which reflect the local plants and animals. Several of the South Sinai protected areas have craft shops run by Bedouin women where their crafts are sold.

In Nabq Protected Area, there lives a seventeen-year-old girl called Salha, who is making her own special contribution to the program. At this early age she has developed into a talented painter and sells her beautiful work to benefit the community and conservation in the area.

EGYPTIAN TORTIOSE PROJECT

PUBLIC AWARNESS PROGRAMS

CAMERA TRAP PROGRAMS

The Egyptian Tortoise, *Testudo kleinmanni,* is a globally endangered species that has become extremely rare in Egypt. Recently a very small population was discovered in Zaranik Protected Area, which became the focus of a multidisciplinary conservation program, 'Tortoise Care,' which aims to secure the future of the species.

This program entails monitoring the wild animals using radio telemetry and traditional tracking methods. Monitoring is carried out almost exclusively by local Bedouin. The program also includes a handcraft component, which encourages local support by bringing economic benefit to the inhabitants of the Protected Area. There are also captive breeding, health screening and public education components to the program.

The EEAA understands the link between sound environmental practice and public awareness and has conducted collaborations on awareness raising with other governmental and non-governmental organizations. Those with the media are so successful that 13 television programs and 35 radio programs on the environment were broadcast in 2000/2001. Additionally, 28 newspapers and magazines regularly carry environmental articles. The EEAA also distributes brochures, video films, CDRoms, and other publications.

Children are key, so in 1998 H.E. Mrs. Suzanne Mubarak launched a program of Green Corner Libraries in which libraries have 'green spaces' where children can learn about nature and the environment.

Camera traps were first deployed in early 1999 in St Katherine Protectorate when six cameras were set up in heatproof boxes. The cameras are equipped with infrared beams and are triggered when an animal passes through the beam, thus breaking it. The program has produced excellent results, with the capture on film of such large mammal species as Striped Hyena, *Hyaena hyaena,* Arabian Wolf, *Canis lupus,* and Blanford's Fox, *Vulpes cana.* Records obtained by means of the program are entered on Geographical Information System (GIS) computers to produce species distribution models.

Today, more people are traveling than ever before and many countries, including Egypt, depend on tourism for a large part, if not the majority, of their income. However, as more tourists visit areas of special natural or cultural interest they place great — sometimes-unsustainable — stress on these sites.

Owing to its aridity, the environment of Egypt is more susceptible to stress than that of many other countries. Therefore, the government is actively promoting the development of eco-tourism as a means of sustainable utilization of fragile habitats, such as the Red Sea reefs, while at the same time generating jobs and providing markets for traditional crafts. Eco-tourism aims to benefit the tourists, the local people and the environment.

The coastal resorts of Egypt are among the fastest growing tourism developments in the world and this is especially true in the protected areas, such as those along the Sinai and Red Sea coasts with their sensitive coral-reef ecosystems. Therefore it was decided to offer various eco-tourism options that would help to underpin the coastal tourism industry. These options are:

- Back country/wilderness – trekking in the mountains
- Eco-archeological tourism – archeological sites, heritage trails
- Religious tourism – treks based on religious sites and routes
- Cultural tourism – learning the secrets of the desert

In addition to these there are:
- Nature safaris – bird watching, nature walks
- Diving – to see the wonderful reefs of the Red Sea

MOUNTAIN TREKKING

DIVING BEDOUIN LODGE

COOPERATION WITH THE INTERNATIONAL COMMUNITY

Cooperation with international organizations has made an important contribution to Egypt's conservation achievements. Over the past decade, the European Union (EU) has supported the development of five protected areas in South Sinai. The outcome of this effort is impressive and has resulted in Egypt's best managed protected areas.

USAID, through the Egyptian Environmental Policy Program (EEPP), is supporting the conservation and management of Red Sea coral reefs and coastal habitats. This involves ongoing coastal management and monitoring efforts and calls for the development of comprehensive management plans for the Red Sea coastal zone, as well as the establishment of new protected areas. The program also has strong public education and information components.

Two projects are carried out in partnership with the government of Italy. One, in Siwa Oasis, involves conservation of natural and cultural heritage including the establishment of a new Protected Area in the region. The other project has established the management structure of Wadi El Rayan Protected Area. Development of the park infrastructure, management and the training of competent personnel are ongoing. The Global Environment Facility (GEF) is supporting the management of three Mediterranean protected areas (El Omayed, Burullus, and Zaranik) and (with UNDP) a project for the conservation and sustainable development of medicinal plants. Most recently a Mangrove rehabilitation project is underway in cooperation with the UN Food and Agriculture Organization (FAO).